I0085033

Pop Culture

Other Works by Davey Beauchamp

Novels

Amazing Pulp Adventures starring Mister Adventure vs the Mysterious Shadow X

Agency 32 the Chelten Affair

Anthologies

Writers for Relief vol. 3

Tales of Fortannis: A Bard in the Hand

Writers for Relief vol. 2

Tales of Fortannis: A Bard's Eye View

Rum and Runestones

Voices for a Cure

Writers for Relief

Other

Davey Beauchamp's Amazing Pulp Adventure RPG

POP CULTURE

A Guide to Getting Teens & Tweens to Read Through
Movies, TV Shows, and Video Games

Davey Beauchamp

POP CULTURE: A Guide to Getting Teens & Tweens to Read Through Movies, TV Shows, and Video Games

Copyright © 2013 by Davey Beauchamp

All rights reserved. No part of this book may be reproduced or transmitted in any form or by any means, electronic or mechanical, including photocopying, recording, or by an information storage and retrieval system - except by a reviewer who may quote brief passages in a review to be printed in a magazine or newspaper - without permission in writing from the publisher.

Publisher's Note: The author and publisher have taken care in the preparation of this book, but make no expressed or implied warranty of any kind and assume no responsibility for errors or omissions. No liability is assumed for incidental or consequential damages in connection with or arising out of the use of the information or programs contained herein.

Published by Sapphire City Press

ISBN-13: 978-0615858593
ISBN-10: 0615858597

Kathleen Duey
For giving me the idea to do this

Dr. Julie Hersberger
For pushing me to becoming the best librarian I could be

Mom
She is my mom

POP CULTURE

A Guide to Getting Teens & Tweens to Read Through
Movies, TV Shows, and Video Games

Table of Contents

Introduction

I never thought I had an original idea when I mentioned on a panel at Dragon*Con how I got books into teens hands. Simply put I use TV Shows, Videos Games, and Movies aka Pop Culture to find books my patrons might enjoy reading.

I thought it was a simple idea which everyone in my field was doing. I had just assumed there were others out there with the same idea I had. I really don't believe this is entirely a new or original idea, but the other panelists along with audience just looked at me like I had said some profound.

I really hadn't.

As I continued to sit on the panel I was still trying to wrap my mind around this. My fellow panelist, author, Kathleen Duey told me I should write a book about how I got books into the hands of teens, along with suggestions and Ideas for people who didn't know TV, film, video games and/or pop culture like I did. I had to think about this, but eventually I decided to write this book/guide/lists of books to help out other Young Adult, Teen, and Tween librarians and educators.

So I hope anyone who uses this guide will mark it up with their own notes in the margins and both agree and disagree with me on my choices. I used what I had in my collection as the foundation of my choices here. I am always open to discussion. I just hope you get something from this endeavor of mine and find it useful in helping your patrons find something to read.

Davey Beauchamp

Here We Go

Getting books into the hands of teens and tweens isn't always the easiest of things to do. Unless of course you just hand them a book and they take it. What this book contains is how I try to get books into their hands; especially when they come to me with the 'I don't know look' on their face or they just flat out tell me they don't have any idea what they want to read, but they have to read something for school.

When this happens I turn to something they do know TV shows, movies and/or video games. I have yet to find a teen who can't tell me at least one of these things they like and have them name a title or two.

As long as I can get them to tell me what sorts of TV shows, movies or video games they like I can a find a book for them. If I can't think of a book off the top of my head; a quick trip to the interwebs and I can.

This book is broken down into three different parts with lists to help those who might not be as fluent in these aspects of pop culture and the books that would go along with them. As you can probably guess the different parts of this book will center around the topics of *TV Shows*, *Movies* and *Video Games*.

Another thing to note is when dealing with Tweens to Teens you are dealing with a wide range of ages and they will all be reading at different levels; with a wide variety of interests.

***

I have been lucky enough to have worked with teens and tweens with every job I have ever had. I have worked in comic book stores, video game stores, and as a fiction author and librarian I have had the chance to go to schools and work with teen's one on one or as a class with creative writing and talking about the publishing world.

The number one thing I have learned when dealing with these younger age groups is not to talk down to them; not to talk to them like they are a big child, but talk to them like they are a person. Talk to them with the same respect you would want them to talk to you with. This attitude works wonders.

If you can talk to a teen about the stuff they know and like such as movies, video games or TV shows. It can show them you aren't the stereo typical librarian they think of when they go to the library, which is the older librarian with a bun on their head and glass telling them to hush and be quite. I would look quite silly with a bun on my head.

Now this book could never teach you about all the stuff going on in the world of pop culture because I am only touching on a fraction of what is considered pop culture here. And honestly pop culture, like the library, is a living breathing organism which is in constant flux and change.

This book will hopefully give you an upper hand in knowing the names of various movies, video games and TV shows that will allow you to find read-a-likes books your younger patrons might like to read.

A key here is never to forget the nonfiction book. These can be just as interesting to teens as anything fiction. Think of all the wonderful biographies of musicians and actors/actress and other people of interest who are out there and books on sports teams. Or a book on a career they might be interested in because they saw an episode of CSI or other TV show or movie.

In the end I hope this book with do a few things:

- Help build a rapport with the teens and tweens that come into your library
- To give you something to help you get the right book in to the hands of your teens to get them interested in a lifetime of reading
- To familiarize yourself with some of the pop culture stuff teens could be into

***

A quick note of how this book is broken down for the ease of use.

This book is broken down first by *Movies*, then *TV Shows* and finally covering *Video Games*. Under each section you will find some of the most popular titles or series. Each series or title will have a brief description of what it is about giving you enough information to think of a book(s) in your library's collection your teen or tween patron might like, but if not; each entry is followed by a list of books, which are of a similar nature or genre.

***

It just hit me as I am writing away; you could use this book to also strike up a conversation with you teens asking them if they have seen movie or TV show X or played video game X, This book could help you open a dialogue of interest with your patrons. Though I would do a tad more research like play the game or watch the movie or an episode or two of the TV shows I have listed, but this is the stuff your teen and tween patrons could be into.

Graphic Novels

You are quickly going to see my love of Comic Books, TPBs, and Graphic Novels in the pages of this book. There is a good reason for that. Most people, especially those who read this book, will not know this, but I am a dyslexic and have a slight speech impediment, a stutter. For those who do know me; very few of them will ever hear the stutter now. It only comes out when I am really, really, tired or very sick.

When I was younger I was taken to a speech therapist and I was diagnosed with what I have. He told my mom the best way for me to beat the dyslexia and the stutter was through reading and he asked me, what were some of my favorite things? And I told him *Star Wars* and *Comic Books*. And I will not lie they are still some of my favorite things to this day. I also have a special place in my two hearts for *Doctor Who* as well.

I still remember parts of that day so well, since I had brought with me my Darth Vader Action Figure Case with all of my Star Wars action figures in it and the therapist had me reading off the names of the characters. And let me tell you some of those character names weren't all that easy to say.

I have been a strong advocate of using comic books to help reluctant teens, tweens, or children to read because they helped me out so much. In the past I have been asked by parents what I liked to read growing up and I tell them story, which leads to comic books.

With me telling them my story and they become quite open to letting their kids try comics books or graphic novels (because there are comics out there for all ages and many now come with a library binding option). From reading comic books I went on to the *Hobbit* and then moved on to the Brian Jacques books to the Weis and Hickman Dragonlance books to becoming an avid reader of all fiction and some nonfiction. I have a B.A. in English with an emphasis in Creative Writing and Professional Writing and a MLIS; along with having published novels, short stories and putting together charity anthologies. And it all started with comic books and Star Wars.

What I am not saying is letting an eight year old read the *Watchmen*, but there is something out there for all ages; like Jeff Smith's *Bone* now being published by Scholastic Books. You just have to look for it and most graphic novels and comics are rated for their attended age groups.

I am going to break down some basic terminology for you.

Graphic Novels – A true graphic novel, the term has been thrown about freely, is an original story produced in trade paperback or hard back book format. The key here it is an original story and not a collection of individual issues of a comic book storyline or mini-series.

Trade Paper Backs (TPBs) – are a collection of individual issues, storylines or mini-series into a single compilation.

Manga – simply but are Japanese comics. And at the time of the writing of this book one of the last two major publishers of manga translated for the United States, TokyoPop, closed down leaving only Viz/Shoen Jump to provide manga to the US and a full of others.

Other things to note in the world of comic books Marvel Comics and DC Comics are considered the two main publishers of mainstream comics.

The major independent publishers who have stood the test of time are Dark Horse Comics, Image Comics, and Archie Comics. One thing to note that most people don't realize is the Archie Comics is one of the oldest independent comic book publishers out there, almost as old as Marvel (Timely) and DC (National) themselves.

As you read through the lists and see any books marked with an asterisk* that means this book is a graphic novel, TPB or manga.

Movies

Welcome to the Movies.

In this section I will try and cover all the big hits over the past couple of years, along with some of the cult classics and what books that the teens in your library might be interested in. By no means will this cover every movie out there, but it should give you a general idea of various themes and genres out there.

Also remember just because a movie is rated "R" or you don't think it is teen or tween appropriate; it doesn't mean they hasn't seen it. So if they ask for something, which is similar to an "R" rated movie, what right do we have to stop them from reading it? Also there always seems to be a YA/Teen equivalent out there for them to read.

Over all movies, in my opinion, can be the hardest thing to use when trying to gage what a teen might like to read and not for content, but for the fact movies come and go so quickly in theaters and then you have all the made for TV movies and straight to DVD releases. So for the purposes here, I am only going to cover movies, which had a theatrical release and were not a made for TV movie or DVD/Blu-Ray release.

I have done my best to use movies here I know my teens have seen, have shown interested in or movies I have shown at my Teen Movie Night. I have also tried to look at what will be coming out in the near future as well and include those films I believe are oriented towards teens.

And another thing I have discovered as my time as a YA Librarian; not all the teens and tweens realize at times their favorite movie(s) are based off of books or series of books. So don't assume the patrons you are dealing with know this fact.

8 Mile

8 Mile is the pseudo true story, fictionalized, of how rapper Eminem rose to fame.

· *Can't Stop Won't Stop: A History of the Hip– Hop Generation* – Chang, Jeff
· *The Way I Am* – Eminem
· *Whatever You Say I Am: The Life and Times of Eminem* – Eminem
· Any biography or book about rappers or the hip– hop industry

9

In the story of *9* the war to end all wars has occurred. The scientist behind the machine which caused the war; uses what is left of his life force to create 9 sack boys and girl to defeat the machine as he seeks redemption for his actions.

· *The City of Ember* – DuPrau, Jeanne
· *Coraline* – Gaiman, Neil
· *The Giver* – Lowry, Lois
· *The Graveyard Book* – Gaiman, Neil
· *The Hunger Games Trilogy* – Collins, Suzanne
· *Shade's Children* – Nix, Garth
· *Vampire Hunter D* – Kikuchi, Hideyuki
· *World War Z: An Oral History of the Zombie War* – Brooks, Max
· *Y: the Last Man vol1. Unmanned** – Vaughan, Brian
· *Z for Zachariah* – O'Brien, Robert

300/300: Rise of an Empire

300 is the story of 300 Spartan warriors who hold the line against the armies of King Xerxes of Persia.

- *300** – Miller, Frank
- *Age of Bronze Volume 1: A Thousand Ship*s* – Shanower, Eric
- *Age of Bronze Volume 2: Sacrifice** – Shanower, Eric
- *Age of Bronze Volume 3: Betrayal Part 1** – Shanower, Eric
- *Mythology* – Hamilton, Edith
- *On Sparta* – Plutarch

Abraham Lincoln Vampire Hunter

In the secret history of America, Abraham Lincoln led a secret life of hunting vampires before and after becoming the president of the United States.

- *Abraham Lincoln, Vampire Hunter* – Grahame-Smith, Seth
- *Alice in Zombieland* – Carroll, Lewis
- *Dracula* – Stoker, Bram
- *iDrakula* – Black Bekka
- *Pride and Prejudice and Zombies* – Hockensmith, Steve
- *Salem's Lot* – King, Stephen
- *Sense and Sensibility and Sea Monsters* – Austin, Jane
- *Vampirates* – Somper, Justin
- *Eighth Grade Bites* – Brewer, Heather

· *Vlad the Impaler: the Real Count Dracula* (Wicked History) – Goldberg, Enid
· *Sterling Biographies Abraham Lincoln: From Pioneer to President* – Phillips, E.B.

Across the Universe

Across the Universe is the story of four friends in the 60s set to the backdrop of the music of the Beatles, the Vietnam War and effects it had on the youth in America.

· *A Hard Day's Write: The Stories Behind Every Beatles Song* – Turner, Steve
· *Fallen Angles* – Myers, Walter Dean
· *Just Listen* – Dessen, Sarah
· *The Land I Lost: Adventures of a Boy in Vietnam*– Huynh, Quang Nhuong
· *Nick and Norah's Infinite Playlist* – Cohn, Rachel & Levithan, David
· *The Wednesday Wars* – Schmidt, Gray
· *Yeah! Yeah! Yeah!: The Beatles, Beatlemania, and the Music that Changed the World* – Spitz, Bob

Akira

Akira is single handedly one of the greatest post futuristic dystopian anime movies to come out of Japan. It is a movie all who are into Japanese Animation (anime) know about. It is the story of teens trying to find their way in the new world order, which appears extremely bleak and mixing in government experimentation in the creation of psychic powers makes for one amazing movie. And one of the coolest futuristic motorcycles ever is in this movie.

· *Akira* Volume 1* – Otomo, Katsuhiro
· *Akira* Volume 2* – Otomo, Katsuhiro
· *Akira* Volume 3* – Otomo, Katsuhiro
· *Akira* Volume 4* – Otomo, Katsuhiro
· *Akira* Volume 5* – Otomo, Katsuhiro
· *Apple Seed* Volume 1* – Masamune, Shirow
· *Battle Royal* – Takami, Koushun
· *Dominion* * – Masamune, Shirow
· *Ghost In the Shell* Volume 1* – Masamune, Shirow
· *Vampire Hunter D Volume 1* * – Kikuchi, Hideyuki
· *Vampire Hunter D Volume 2* *– Kikuchi, Hideyuki
· *Vampire Hunter D Volume 3* *– Kikuchi, Hideyuki
· *Vampire Hunter D* (Novels/Series) – Kikuchi, Hideyuki

Alice in Wonderland

This is Tim Burton's twisted view of Alice in Wonderland. Alice is now a grown woman and must once again return to Wonderland to discover just who she is, while finally put an end to the Queen of Hearts.

· *Alice in Wonderland* – Carol, Lewis
· *The Annotated Alice* – Carol, Lewis
· *Chronicles of Narnia* – Lewis, C.S.
· *Coraline* – Gaiman, Neil
· *Darwen Arkwright and the Insidious Bleck* – Hartley, A.J.
· *Darwen Arkwright and the Peregrine Pact* – Hartley, A.J.

· *Peter Pan* – Barrie, J.M.
· *Through the Looking Glass* – Carol, Lewis
· *The Wonderful Wizard of Oz* – Baum, L. Frank
· *American McGee's Grimm** - Macpherson, Dwight

The Alien Saga (Alien, Aliens, Aliens 3, Aliens 4: Resurrection)

The Alien saga at its core it man vs. alien. These aliens are not the cute E.T. or Grey types. These aliens are mean killing machines that adapt and gain aspects from the life form in which they are spawned from.

· *Aliens Omnibus, Vol. 1** – Verheiden, Mark
· *Aliens Omnibus, Vol. 2** – Various
· *Aliens Omnibus, Vol. 3** – Edington, Ian
· *Aliens Omnibus, Vol. 4** – Various
· *Aliens Omnibus, Vol. 5** – Arcudi, John
· *It* – King, Stephen
· *Predator Omnibus Vol. 1** – Verheiden, Mark
· *War of the Worlds* – Wells, H.G.

Anne of Green Gables

This is a story of a young orphan girl mistakenly sent to Prince Edward Island to help a brother and sister out on their farm. This is about her adventures on Green Gables.

· *Anne of Green Gables* – Montgomery, Lucy
· *Anne of Avonlea* – Montgomery, Lucy

- *Anne of the Island* – Montgomery, Lucy
- *Anne of Windy Poplars* – Montgomery, Lucy
- *Anne's House of Dreams* – Montgomery, Lucy
- *Anne of Ingleside* – Montgomery, Lucy
- *Little House on the Prairie* – Wilder, Laura
- *Little Women* – Alcott, Louisa
- *Little Princess* – Burnett, Frances

Avatar

Avatar delves into the planetary colonization for wealth where the all indigenous life is all connected to one another. In order to make peace with the Navi, the intelligent life forms, the humans have created avatar bodies that look like the Navi. Things go from bad to worse as war breaks out between the Navi and humans.

- *Dune* – Herbert, Frank
- *Ender's Game* – Card, Orson Scott
- *On Basilisk Station* – Weber, David
- *A Princess of Mars* – Burroguhs, Edgar Rice
- *Starship Troopers* – Heinlein, Robert

The Avengers

Marvel brings forth all their big guns into one single movie, just as the comics books did back in the 60s. This movie features Captain America, Thor, and Iron-Man along with a whole host of other heroes to form the Mighty Avengers.

· *The Avengers, Vol. 1* (Marvel Masterworks)* – Lee, Stan
· *Avengers, Vol. 1** – Bendis, Brian Michael
· *Avengers Assemble, Vol. 1** – Busiek, Kurt
· *Avengers: The Contest** – Mantlo, Bill
· *Avengers Disassembled** – Bendis, Brian Michael
· *New Avengers, Vol. 1** – Bendis, Brian Michael
· *Hulk: Gray** – Loeb, Jeph
· *Marvels** – Busiek, Kurt

Batman

Batman, Bruce Wayne, is haunted by the deaths of his parents and uses the family fortune to become the Dark Knight. In doing so he is trying to make the streets of Gotham City safe from gangs, criminals, and costumed villains of all shapes, sizes, and sanities.

· *Artemis Fowl* – Colfer, Eoin
· *Batman: Arkham Asylum** – Morrison, Grant
· *Batman Chronicles, Vol. 1** – Kane, Bob
· *Batman: Dead White* – Shirley, John
· *Batman the Dark Knight Returns** – Miller, Frank
· *Batman: Earth One** – Johns, Geoff
· *Batman: Fear Itself* – Reaves, Michael

- *Batman: Inferno* – Irvine, Alex
- *Batman: The Long Halloween** – Loeb, Jeph
- *Batman and Me* – Kane, Bob
- *Batman: No Man's Land* – Rucka, Greg
- *Batman the World of the Dark Knight* – Wallace, Daniel
- *Batman: Year One* – Miller, Frank
- *Wayne of Gotham* – Hickman, Tracy

Beautiful Creatures

A new girl comes to the town of Gatlin and quickly catches the eye of Ethan who wants to escape the small, dead end, town. The two uncover a dark secret about their two families and the town.

- *Beautiful Creatures* (book 1) – Garcia, Kami
- *Beautiful Darkness* (book 2) – Garcia, Kami
- *Beautiful Chaos* (book 3) – Garcia, Kami
- *Beautiful Redemption* (book 4) – Garcia, Kami
- *Beautiful Creatures** (manga) – Garcia, Kami
- *Hush, Hush* – Fitzpatrick, Becca
- *City of Bones* – Clare, Cassandra

Beastly

A modern day retelling of *Beauty and the Beast*; Kyle, the rich popular kid, asks out the goth girl who he then blows off cruelly. She then curses Kyle, which disfigures his appearance and must find true love in order to lift the curse.

- *Beast* – Napoli, Donna Jo
- *Beastly* – Finn, Alex
- *Beauty and the Beast* – Various
- *Beauty: A Retelling of the Story of Beauty and the Beast* – McKinley
- *Cloaked* – Finn, Alex
- *A Kiss in Time* – Finn, Alex
- *Wicked* – Maguire, Gregory
- *Indelible* – Metcalf, Dawn
- *Of Beast and Beauty* – Jacy, Stacey

The Blind Side

This is the story of Michael Oher, NFL Left Tackle and how the kindness of a stranger and her family changed his life forever from giving him a home when he had none and a chance to better himself, which lead to a life in the NFL.

- *The Blind Side: Evolution of a Game* – Lewis, Michael
- *Catch that Pass!* – Christopher, Matt
- *Every Play Every Day: My Life as a Notre Dame Walk-on* – O'Neill, Timmy
- *Football Double Threat* – Christopher, Matt · *Football Nightmare* – Christopher, Matt

· *Friday Night Lights: A Town, a Team, and a Dream* –
Bissinger, Buzz
· *The Great Quarterback Switch* – Christopher, Matt
· *I Beat the Odds: From Homelessness, the The Blind Side, and Beyond* – Oher, Michael
· *No More Dead Dogs* – Korman, Gordon
· *On the Field with... Peyton and Eli Manning* –
Christopher, Matt
· *Remember This Titan: the Bill Yoast Story* – Sullivan
· *Tough to Tackle* – Christopher, Matt

The Boy in the Striped Pajamas

Setting during War World II; the son of a German officer forms a friendship with a young Jewish boy on the other side of a fence of a concentration camp.

· *The Book Thief* – Zusak, Markus
· *The Boy in the Striped Pajamas* – Boyne, John
· *Diary of Young Girl* – Frank, Anne
· *I Have Lived A Thousand Years* – Bitton-Jackson, Livia
· *In the Camps* – Axelrod, Toby
· *MAUS I & II** – Spiegelman, Art
· *Number the Stars* – Lowry, Lois
· *We are Witnesses* – Boas, Jacob

Brave

Merida, a Scottish Princess, wants more out of life than the lot she was cast. Through a witch's spell she gets her wish granted and more. It throws her and the kingdom's world into chaos. Now she must choose between the world she once knew and the world created by the witch's spell.

· *The Art of Brave* – Lerew, Jenny
· *Brave Junior Novelization* – Trimble, Irene
· *Cinderella* – Various
· *The Demon Trapper's Daughter: A Demon Trappers Novel* – Oliver, Jana
· *Dragonriders of Pern* (series) – McCaffrey, Anne
· *The Legacy of Tril: Soulbound* – Brewer, Heather
· *The Little Mermaid* – Anderson, Hans Christian
· *The Lore of Scotland: A Guide to Scottish Legends* – Westwood, Jennifer
· *Soul Thief: A Demon Trappers Novel* – Oliver, Jana
· *Tangled: the Junior Novelization* – Trimble, Irene
· *War of the Seasons, Book Two: The Half-blood* – Spendlove, Janine
· *War of the Seasons, Book One: The Human* – Spendlove, Janine
· *Wonder Woman, Vol. 1: Blood** - Azzarello, Brian
· *Wonder Woman Vol. 2: Guts** - Azzarello, Brian
· *Wonder Woman Vol. 3: Iron** - Azzarello, Brian

Bridge to Terabithia

The *Bridge to Terabithia* is the story of two friends who create an imaginary world together filled with all things fantasy. In the end the real world and life comes crashing in upon them.

- *Bridge to Terabithia – Paterson*, Katherine
- *Chronicles of Narnia – Lewis*, C.S.
- *Howl's Moving Castle – Jones*, Diana
- *Island of the Blue Dolphins – O'Dell*, Scott
- *A Wrinkle in Time – L'Engle*, Madeleine

Captain America/Captain America 2 Winter Solider

The year is 19 41 and Steve Rodgers, 98 pound weakling, is given an experimental serum to transform him in a super solider. He was supposed to be the first of many but when the scientist behind the super solider is assassinated; Captain America was born.

- *Avengers, Vol. 1.** – Lee, Stan
- *Captain America, Vol. 1* (Marvel Masterworks)* – Lee, Stan
- *Captain America: The Chosen** – Morrell, David
- *Captain America: Rebirth** – Waid, Mark
- *Captain America: Reborn** – Brubaker, Ed
- *Captain America, Vol. 1 Winter Solider** – Brubaker, Ed
- *Captain America, Vol. 2 Winter Solider** – Brubaker, Ed
- *The Death of Captain America** – Brubaker, Ed
- *Marvel Masterworks: Golden Age Captain America, Vol. 1* – Simon, Joe
- *Marvel Comics: The Untold Story* – Howe, Sean

Charlie and the Chocolate Factory

A very poor child, Charlie, has his world flipped upside down when he discovers a golden ticket in his Wonka bar, which might change his life and the life of his family forever. As long as he can pass a secret test put in place by the great candy maker himself, Willy Wonka.

· *Charlie and the Chocolate Factory* – Dahl, Roald
· *Charlie and the Great Glass Elevator* – Dahl, Roald
· *James and the Giant Peach* – Dahl, Roald
· Lemony Snicket Series – Snicket, Lemony
· *Matilda* – Dahl, Roald
· *Stuart Little* – White, E.B.
· *Secret Garden* – Burnett, Frances

Chronicles of Narnia (*The Lion the Witch and the Wardrobe, Prince Caspin, Voyage of the Dawn Treader*)

An epic tale surrounding the Pevensie family as they travel between war-torn England and mystical/fantasy filled land of Narnia. This is an adventure of war, mythical and mystic creatures, exploration and self-discovery with Christian overtones.

· *Chronicles of Narnia* – Lewis, C.S.
· *Companion to Narnia, Revised Edition: A Complete Guide to the Magical World of C.S. Lewis's The Chronicles of Narnia* – Ford, Paul
· *Darwen Arkwright and the Insidious Bleck* – Hartley, A.J.
· *Darwen Arkwright and the Peregrine Pact* – Hartley, A.J.

· *Darwen Arkwright and the School of Shadows* – Hartley, A.J.
· *The Hobbit* – Tolkien, J.R. R.
· *The Wonderful Wizard of Oz* – Baum, L. Frank
· *Wizard of Earthsea* – Le Guin, Ursula
· *A Wrinkle in Time* – L'Engle, Madeleine

Clash of the Titans/Wrath of the Titans

This movie is loosely based on the Greek myth of Perseus. Perseus, son of Zeus, is determined to save the city of Argos, Princess Andromeda and to put the Gods and Goddess of Olympus in their place. While Hades uses the turmoil to try and seize the throne of Olympus for himself.

· *Goddess of Yesterday* – Cooney, Caroline
· *The Greek Way* – Hamilton, Edith
· *The Heroes of Olympus* – Riordan, Rick
· *The Iliad* – Homer
· *Mythology* – Hamilton, Edith
· *Odyssey* – Homer
· *Percy Jackson and the Lightening Thief* – Riordan, Rick
· *The Red Pyramid* – Riordan, Rick
· *The Roman Way* – Hamilton, Edith
· *Sirena* – Napoli, Donna
· *Wonder Woman, Vol. 1: Blood** - Azzarello, Brian
· *Wonder Woman Vol. 2: Guts** - Azzarello, Brian

Cloverfield

Cloverfield is the American equivalent of Godzilla. Monster destroys New York City from the perspective of a group of friends trying to find their loved ones before they are killed by the monster's rampage.

· *The Call of Cthulhu and Other Weird Stories* – Lovecraft, H.P.
· *Daikaiju! Giant Monster Tales* – Hood, Robert
· *Daikaiju!2 Revenge of the Giant Monsters* – Hood, Robert
· *Daikaiju!3 Giant Monsters vs the World* – Hood, Robert
· *Godzilla Age of Monsters** – Stradley, Randy
· *Godzilla on My Mind: Fifty Years of the King of Monsters* – Tsutsui, William
· *Monstrous: 20Tales of Giant Creature Terror* – Thomas, Ryan

Confessions of a Teenage Drama Queen

A girl from New York City moves to small city in New Jersey and wants to reclaim her title she had in her old high school as the most popular girl in school.

· *Confessions of a Teenage Drama Queen* – Sheldon, Dyan
· *How Not to Be Popular* – Ziegler, Jennifer
· *Mates, Date, and … Series* – Hopkins, Cathy
· *My Perfect Life* – Sheldon, Dyan
· *The Summer I Became a Nerd* – Miller, Leah Rae

Coraline

Coraline is the story of a girl who wants something different and travels to an odd world which mimics her own and is strangely twisted, but what seems wonderful at first turns into a nightmare. And in the end all Coraline wants to do is return home to her own world.

· *Alice in Wonderland* – Carol, Lewis
· *The Bad Beginning* – Snicket, Lemony
· *Coraline*: the Graphic Novel* – Gaiman, Neil
· *Chronicles of Narnia* – Lewis, C.S.
· *Darwen Arkwright and the Insidious Bleck* – Hartley, A.J.
· *Neverwhere* – Gaiman, Neil
· *Peter Pan* – Barrie, J.M.
· *Through the Looking Glass* – Carol, Lewis
· *The Wonderful Wizard of Oz* – Baum, L. Frank

Despicable Me (series)

Mad Scientist/Evil Genius turns good when he adopts three orphaned girls and they open the door to fatherhood; something he never imagined he had inside of him.

· *Artemis Fowl* – Colfer, Eoin
· *Artemis Fowl: The Artic Incident* – Colfer, Eoin
· *Artemis Fowl: The Eternity Code* – Colfer, Eoin
· *Artemis Fowl: The Opal Deception* – Colfer, Eoin
· *Artemis Fowl: The Lost Colony* – Colfer, Eoin
· *Artemis Fowl: The Time Paradox* – Colfer, Eoin
· *Artemis Fowl: The Atlantis Complex* – Colfer, Eoin

· *Artemis Fowl: The Last Guardian* – Colfer, Eoin
· *The Bad Beginning & Lemony Snicket Series* – Snicket, Lemony
· *Evil Genius* – Jinks, Catherine
· *The Hunchback Assignments* (series) – Slade, Arthur

Diary of a Wimpy Kid (series)

Kid enters middle school and must survive the obstacles set before him in the way of morns, bullies, teachers and the ever dreaded cooties.

· *Diary of a Wimpy Kid* – Kinney, Jeff
· *Rodrick Rules* – Kinney, Jeff
· *The Last Straw* – Kinney, Jeff
· *Dog Days*– Kinney, Jeff
· *The Ugly Truth* – Kinney, Jeff
· *Cabin Fever* – Kinney, Jeff
· *The Third Wheel* – Kinney, Jeff
· *How to Eat Fried Worms* – Rockwell, Thomas
· *Middle School* series – Patterson, James
· *The Strange Case of Origami Yoda* – Angleberger, Tom
· *Darth Paper Strikes Back: An Origami Yoda Book* – Angleberger, Tom
· *The Secret Fortune Wookie: An Origami Yoda Book* – Angleberger, Tom
· *The Surprise Attack of Jabba the PuppettL An Origami Yoda Book* – Angleberger, Tom
· *Dork Diaries* series – Russell, Rachel
· *Big Nate* series – Peirce Lincoln

Die Hard (series)

Cop John McClain never seems to have a normal holiday. They always tend to lead to terroristic threats, which he must defuse and save the day.

· *Alex Rider* Series – Horowitz, Anthony
· *Henderson's Boys* Series – Muchamore, Robert
· *Dirk Pitt Adventures* – Cussler, Clive
· *Nothing Lasts Forever* – Roderick, Thorp
· *The Young Bond* Series – Higson, Charlie

District 9

Aliens arrive on Earth and are in need of our help, but instead of helping them; the aliens are put into camps and contained.

· *The Host* – Stephenie Meyer
· *Starship Troopers* – Heinlein, Robert
· *V: The Original Miniseries* – Johnson, Kenneth
· *V: The Second Generation* – Johnson, Kenneth
· *The War of the Worlds* – Wells, H.G.
· *I Am Number Four* – Lore, Pittacus
· *Ender's Game* – Card, Orson Scott

Ella Enchanted

Princess tend to blessed by their Fairy God parents at birth; not this time. Ella is given the gift of absolute obedience.

· *Ella Enchanted* – Levine, Gail
· *The Two Princesses of Bamarre* – Levine, Gail
· *Fairest* – Levine Gail
· *Beauty: A Retelling of the Story of Beauty and the Beast* – McKinley
· *Just Ella* – Haddix, Margaret

Ender's Game

Humanity has turn to children to win a war against an alien race. Ender Wiggin must fight a desperate battle for mankind to survive this threat.

· *Ender's Game* – Card, Orson Scott
· *Speaker for the Dead* – Card, Orson Scott
· *Xenocide* – Card, Orson Scott
· *Children of the Mind* – Card, Orson Scott
· *Ender's Shadow* – Card, Orson Scott
· *Shadow of the Hegemon* – Card, Orson Scott
· *Shadow Puppets* – Card, Orson Scott
· *First Meetings* – Card, Orson Scott
· *Shadow of the Giant* – Card, Orson Scott
· *A War of Gifts: An Ender Story* – Card, Orson Scott
· *Ender in Exile* – Card, Orson Scott
· *Shadows in Flight* – Card, Orson Scott

- *Earth Unaware* – Card, Orson Scott
- *Earth Afire* – Card, Orson Scott
- *Shadows Alive* – Card, Orson Scott
- *A Beautiful Friendship* (Star Kingdom) – Weber, David
- *Shadows Alive* (Star Kingdom) – Weber, David
- *Starship Troopers* – Heinlein, Robert

E.T.: the Extra –Terrestrial

An alien is left on planet Earth. Said alien meets a boy and become friends. Boy must help the alien contact his home before the government finds the alien and kill him.

- *Across the Universe* – Revis, Veronica
- *Aliens Encounters with the Unexplained* – Day, Marcus
- *Dead Strange the Bizarre Truths Behind 50 World-Famous Mysteries* – Lamy, Matt
- *E.T.: THE EXTRA-TERRESTRIAL* – Koztwinkle, William
- *E.T.: The Book of the Green Planet: A Novel* – Kotzwinkle, William
- *I Am Number Four* (Lorien Legacies) – Lore, Pittacus
- *Unexplained: Curious Phenomena, Strange, Superstitions, and Ancient Mysteries* – Allen, Judy

Fast and the Furious Saga (the Fast and the Furious, 2 Fast 2 Furious, the Fast and Furious: Tokyo Drift, Fast & Furious, Fast and Furious 5, Furious 6)

Fast cars, adventures, and who is the bad guy and who is the good guy? The lines of are blurred as street racing, murders, drugs and whole lot action are brought together all over the world.

- *Initial D Vol. 1** – Shigeno, Shuichi
- *Christine* – King, Stephen
- *Saturday Night Dirt* – Weaver, Will
- *The Physics of NASCAR: How to Make Steel + Gas + Rubber = Speed* – Leslie– Pelecky, Diandra
- *Slide or Die (Drift X)* * – Strasser, Todd
- *Speed Racer & Racer X: The Origins Collection* – Yune, Tommy
- *Super Stock Rookie* – Weaver, Will

Field of Dreams

A man tries to reconnect to his father with the famous line, "If you build it, he will come." A man buys a farm and he is compelled to build baseball field in the middle of his corn field. In some circles this is considered one of the best Baseball movies ever made.

- *Eight Men Out: The Black Sox and the 1919 World Series* – Asinof, Eliot
- *The Natural* – Malamud, Bernard
- *Samurai Shortstop* – Gratz, Alan
- *Shoeless Joe* – Kinsella, W.P.
- *Summerland* – Chabon, Michael

Fight Club

Anarchy, insanity, and the first rule of Fight Club is that you don't talk about Fight Club. A man loses his mind as his new best friend is a figment of his own imagination, which takes control of him sending him on an adventure to bring down the capitalistic society of America.

· *Battle Royal* – Takami, Koushun
· *A Clockwork Orange* – Burgess, Anthony
· *Fight Club* – Palahniuk, Chuck
· *Lord of the Flies* – Golding, William
· *The Picture of Dorian Gray* – Wilde, Oscar
· *The Strange Case of Dr Jekyll and Mr Hyde* – Stevenson, Robert Louis
· *Stranger in a Strange Land* – Heinlein, Robert
· *V for Vendetta** – Moore, Alan

Freaky Friday

Daughter and mother switch bodies and experience life in each other's shoes. Wacky misadventures occur as each one ties to live the other's life.

· *Freaky Friday* – Rodgers, Mary
· *Freaky Monday* – Rodgers, Mary
· *How to Eat Fried Worms* – Rockwell, Thomas
· *Lunchroom Wars* – Emerson, Marcus
· *Summer Switch* – Rodgers, Mary

Friday the 13th Series

Serial Killer/Monster, Jason Voorhees, stalks the woods around Camp Crystal Lake. The first time around it was Jason's mother. After that it was the supernaturally reanimated corpse of Jason.

· *Acceleration* – McNamee, Graham
· *The Body Finder* – Derting, Kimberly
· *Christopher Killer* – Ferguson, Alane
· *Darkly Dreaming Dexter* – Lindsay, Jeff
· *Fear Street* Series – Stein, L.R.
· *I Am Not a Serial Killer* – Wells, Dan
· *I Know What You Did Last Summer* – Duncan, Lois
· *The Strange Case of Dr Jekyll and Mr. Hyde* – Stevenson, Robert Louis
· *A Midsummer Night's Scream* – Stein, R.L.

Ghostbusters

Four men, three scientists and an everyday Joe, band together to deal with ghosts haunting New Yotk City. This leads to a confrontation with a Samarian God in the form of the Stay Puff Marshmellow Man.

· *The Awakening* – Gibson, Mar-58ley
· *Ghostbusters: Haunted Holidays** – Naraghi, Dara
· *Ghostbusters: The Other Side** – Champagne, Keith
· *Ghosts* – Parks, Peggy
· *The Graveyard Book* – Gaiman, Neil
·*Haunted* – Cabot, MEg

- *The Other Side: A Teen's Guide to Ghost Hunting and the Paranormal* – Gibson, Marley
- *Poltergeists* – Kallen, Stuart

GI Joe: the Rise of Cobra /GI Joe: Retaliation

GI Joe is an elite fighting force, made up of men and women from around the world, protecting the world from the evil forces of the terrorist organization Cobra. This entry is also good for any GI Joe based cartoon show on television.

- *Classic G.I. Joe Vol.1** – Hama, Larry
- *G.I. Joe Volume 1** – Dixon, Chuck
- *G.I. Joe: Cobra** – Gage, Christos
- *G.I. Joe: Hearts & Minds, A G.I. Joe Graphic Novel** – Brooks, Max
- *G.I. Joe Special Missions Vol.1** – Hama, Larry
- *G.I. Joe: Tales from the Cobra Wars** – Brooks, Max

The Girl with the Dragon Tattoo Trilogy aka The Millennium Trilogy (The Girl with Dragon Tattoo, The Girl Who Played With Fire, The Girl Who Kicked the Hornet's Nest) (Both Foreign and Domestic Films)

A girl with a tormented past finally takes control of her life as she discovers that there were forces beyond her control shaping her life for the worse thanks to her father and the political connections he had.

- *Brainjack* – Falkner Brian

- *Genius Squad* – Jinks, Catherine
- *The Girl Who Kicked the Hornet's Nest* – Larsson, Stieg
- *The Girl Who Played With Fire* – Larsson, Stieg
- *The Girl With the Dragon Tattoo* – Larsson, Stieg
- *Hunger Games: Trilogy* – Collins, Suzan
- *Neuromancer* – Gibson, William

Godzilla

Godlzilla, king of Kaiju monsters, destroys Tokyo or battles other giant Kaiju monsters time and time again.

- *The Call of Cthulhu and Other Weird Stories* – Lovecraft, H.P.
- *Godzilla Age of Monsters** – Stradley, Randy
- *Godzilla: Half Century War** – Stoke, James
- *Godzilla: Kingdom of Monsters Volume 1** – Powell, Eric
- *Godzilla: Legends** – Frank, Matt
- *Godzilla Volume 1** - Swierczynski, Duane
- *Godzilla on My Mind: Fifty Years of the King of Monsters* – Tsutsui, William
- *Pacific Rim: The Official Movie Novelization* – Irvine, Alexander
- *Pacific Rim: Man, Machines, and Monsters* – Cohen, David
- *Evangelion* (series) – Sadamoto, Yoshiyuki

The Golden Compass

The Golden Compass is part of the *His Dark Materials* series. It is about a girl who does not know she is destined to bring balance to her world, while trying to overcome adverse odds who would see this not happen.

- *The Amber Spyglass* – Pullman, Philip
- *Behemoth* – Westerfeld, Scott
- *The Golden Compass* – Pullman, Philip
- *Goliath* Westerfeld, Scott
- *Howl's Moving Castle* – Jones, Diana
- *Leviathan* – Westerfeld, Scott
- *Mortal Engines* – Reeve, Philip
- *The Subtle Knife* – Pullman, Philip

Goonies

The misadventures of a group of kids (the Goonies) trying to save their home town as they seek the lost pirate treasure of One Eyed Willy and stay one step ahead of the Fratellis Family.

- *Cirque du Freak* – Shan, Darren
- *Harry Potter and the Sorcerer's Stone* – Rowling, J.K.
- *House of Secrets* – Columbus, Chris
- *Peter Pan* – Barrie, J.M.
- *Peter and the Starcatchers* – Barry, Dave
- *Three Weeks with The Goonies: On Location in Astoria, Oregon* – Alderman, Mick
- *Treasure Island* – Stevenson, Robert Louis

The Great Gatsby

F. Scott Fitzgerald's master piece brought to the Silver Screen. This is a love story gone horribly wrong set to the back of the roaring 20s. No one gets through this story unscathed.

· *F. Scott Fitzgerald* – Bloom's BioCritiques
· *F. Scott Fitzgerald Writer of the Jazz Age* – Brackett, Virginia
· *The Flappers* (series) – Larkin, Jillian
· *The Great Gatsby* – Fitzgerald, F. Scott
· *Through No Fault of My Own: A Girl's Diary of Life on Summit Avenue in the Jazz Age* – Irvine, Coco
· *Diviners* – Libba, Bray

Green Lantern

In brightest day and darkest night, no evil shall escape my sight, let those who worship evil's might beware my power... Green Lantern's Light! Hal Jordan is chosen to become the Guardian of Sector of 2814 and part of the Green Lantern Corps when Abin Sur crashes on Earth and dies.

· Brightest Day Vol. 1* – Johns, Geoff
· Blackest Night*– Johns, Geoff
· Green Lantern Origins* – Johns, Geoff
· Green Lantern: Blackest Night*– Johns, Geoff
· Green Lantern, Vol. 1: No Fear*– Johns, Geoff
· Green Lantern Rebirth*– Johns, Geoff
· Green Lantern: The Sinestro Corps. Vol.1* – Johns, Geoff

· The Green Lantern Chronicles * – Broome, John
· Green Lantern Corps Vol. 1: To Be a Lantern* – Gibbons, Dave
· Green Lantern: Emerald Warriors, vol.1* – Tomasi, Peter
· Showcase Presents: Green Lantern, Vol. 5* – O'Neil, Denny
· Tales of the Green Lantern Corps, Vol. 1*– Various

Guardians of the Galaxy

A rag tag team of alien beings (a living tree, a raccoon, and a daughter of ruthless killer) led by an Earthman (Peter Quill aka the Star Lord) save the universe against over whelming odds. This is another part of the Marvel Movie Universe.

· *Guardians of the Galaxy, Vol. 1: Cosmic Avengers* – Bendis, Brian
· *Guardians of the Galaxy: Tomorrow's Avengers - Vol. 1* – Gerber, Steve
· *Guardians of the Galaxy, Vol. 1: Legacy* – Abnett, Dan
· *Nova, Vol. 1: Origin* – Loeb, Jeph
· *Thanos Rising* – Aaron, Jason
· *Infinity Gauntlet* – Starlin, Jim

Hansel and Gretel: Witch Hunters

After Hansel and Gretel survived their encounter with the witch, they became witch hunters. This time they come up against something that might be something more monstrous than witches.

- *Fables Vol. 1: Legends in Exile* – Willingham, Bill
- *Grimm's Fairy Tales* – Brother's Grimm
- *Grimm - The Icy Touch* – Shirley, John
- *The Savage Tales of Solomon Kane* – Howard, Robert E.
- *The Scourge of Jericho (the Witch Hunter Chronicles)* – Daly Stuart
- *Twisted Fairy Tales* – McHugh, Maura

Harry Potter Saga (*Harry Potter and the Sorcerer's Stone, Harry Potter and the Chamber of Secrets, Harry Potter and the Prisoner of Azkaban, Harry Potter and the Goblet of Fire, Harry Potter and the Order of the Phoenix, Harry Potter and the Half Blood Prince, Harry Potter and the Deathly Hallows Pt. 1, Harry Potter and the Deathly Hallows Pt. 2*)

An orphan discovers that he is much more that he appears and scar on his forehead is his legacy. Set in a world of magic that exists in parallel to the real world, but hidden from it as well. This is the classic battle between good and evil along with a coming of age story that one day will hopefully a modern classic.

- *Harry Potter and the Sorcerer's Stone* – Rowling, J.K.
- *Harry Potter and the Chamber of Secrets*– Rowling, J.K.
- *Harry Potter and the Prisoner of Azkaban* – Rowling, J.K.
- *Harry Potter and the Goblet of Fire*– Rowling, J.K.

· *Harry Potter and the Order of the Phoenix* – Rowling, J.K.
· *Harry Potter and the Half Blood Prince* – Rowling, J.K.
· *Harry Potter and the Deathly Hallows* – Rowling, J.K.
· *The Tales of Beedle the Bard* – Rowling, J.K.
· *Lord of the Ring: Fellowship of the Ring* – Tolkien, J.R.R.
· *The Hobbit* – Tolkien, J.R.R.
· *Jonathan Strange &Mr. Norrell* – Clarke, Susanna
· *Good Omens* – Gaiman, Neil

Hellboy

During WWII the Nazis try to bring about the end of the world by summoning a demon from Hell, but instead they are interrupted by American fighting forces. What comes through is a baby demon, Hellboy, who is raised by the Americans. Hellboy now helps combat supernatural threats and terrors.

· *Abe Sapien: The Drowing** – Mignola, Mike
· *Baltimore,: Or, The Steadfast Tin Solider and the Vampire* – Mignola, Mike
· *B.P.R.D., Vol.1: Hollow Earth & Other Stories** – *Mignola*, Mike
· *B.P.R.D., Vol.2: The Soul of Venice & Other Stories** – *Mignola*, Mike
· *Faust: A Tragedy* – Wolfgang von Goethe, Johann
· *Hellboy, Vol.1: Seeds of Destruction** – Mignola, Mike
· *Hellboy Vol.2: Wake the Devil** – *Mignola*, Mike
· *Monster Hunter International* – Larry Correia
· *Witchfinder: In the Service of Angels* – *Mignola*, Mike

The Hitchhiker's Guide to the Galaxy

Don't Panic. The Earth is destroyed to make way for an intergalactic space way. Arthur Dent is the last surviving human man; thanks in part to his friend and alien Ford Prefect. Arthur is now traveling with Ford to find his place in the Universe and along for the ride is the last human woman, whom he happened to meet at a costume party, a two headed alien, and an ever depressed robot Marvin. So don't panic or forget your towel.

· *The Hitchhiker's Guide to the Galaxy* – Adams, Douglas
· *The Restaurant at the End of the Universe* – Adams, Douglas
· *Life the Universe and Everything* – Adams, Douglas
· *So Long, and Thanks for All the Fish* – Adams, Douglas
· *Mostly Harmless* – Adams, Douglas
· *And Another Thing* – Colfer, Eoin
· *Doctor Who: Shada: the Lost Adventure by Douglas Adams* – Roberts, Gareth
· *Good Omens: The Nice and Accurate Prophecies of Agnes Nutter, Witch* – Gaiman, Neil
· *The Salmon of Doubt: Hitchhiking the Galaxy One Last Time* – Adams, Douglas
· *Starship Titanic* – Adams, Douglas

The Hobbit (both the Live Action and Animated)

Bilbo Baggins goes on a journey that will change his life forever. From Dwarves to Trolls to Dragons and a wizard a simple Hobbit will change the world of Middle Earth forever, in this prologue to the Lord of the Rings.

· *The Black Cauldron* – Alexander, Lloyd
· *Dragons of Autumn Twilight* – Weis, Margaret
· *The Hobbit* – Tolkien, J.R.R.
· *The Hobbit** – Dixon, Charles
· *Guards! Guards!* – Practchett, Terry
· *The Last Unicorn* – Beagle, Peter
· *Lord of the Rings* – Tolkien, J.R.R.
· *Mossflower (Redwall, Book 2)* – Jacques, Brain
· *The Ruins of Gorlan (the Ranger's Apprentice, Book 1)* – Flanagan, John

Holes

Stanley is wrongfully accused of stealing a pair of sneakers and is sent to Camp Green Lake. He, along with the other kids sent there, are forced to dig holes in a long dried up lake. The warden is hoping they will discover a long lost treasure.

· *Boot Camp* – Strasser, Todd
· *Holes* – Sachar, Louis
· *Hoot* – Hiaasen, Carl
· *The Lightening Thief* – Riordan, Rick
· *The Outcasts of 19 Schuyler Place* - Konigsburg, E.L.
· *Treasure Island* – Stevenson, Robert Louis

The Host

The world has been taken over by aliens who have taken over our own bodies. Normal humans only exist in small groups scattered to the remote areas. Then came Melanie possessed by Wander. It is more of a symbiotic relationship then one of control. Now it is up to them to bridge the gap between humans and the aliens.

- *Childhood's End* – Clarke, Arthur C.
- *Dreamcatcher* – King, Stephen
- *The Giver* – Lowery
- *Invasion of the Body Snatchers* – Finney, Jack
- *Uglies* – Westerfeld, Scott
- *War of the Worlds* – Wells, H.G.

Howl's Moving Castle

A young girl is cursed and becomes an old woman. Her road to freedom from the curse leads her to a very curious wizard, Howl, who lives many mysterious lives and who resides in a moving castle.

- *Howl's Moving Castle* – Jones, Diana · *Castle in the Air* – Jones, Diana
- *House of Many Ways* – *Jones*, Diana
- *Wizard's Castle* – *Jones*, Diana
- *Sorcery and Cecelia, or, The Enchanted Chocolate Pot* – Stevermer, Caroline
- *Howl's Moving Castle Film Comic, Vol.1* – Miyazaki, Hayao

· *Howl's Moving Castle Picture Book* – Miyazaki, Hayao
· *Stardust* – Gaiman, Neil

Hulk

Dr. Bruce Banner is hit by a massive dose of Gamma Radiation transforming him in the Hulk. He is now being hunted by General Thunderbolt Ross the father of the Betty Ross, Banner's love.

· *The Avengers, Vol. 1* (Marvel Masterworks)* – Lee, Stan
· *Hulk: Gray** – Loeb, Jeph
· *Incredible Hulk: Planet Hulk** – Pak*, Greg
· *Incredible Hulk Vol.1* (Marvel Masterworks)* – Lee, Stan
· *Incredible Hulk: The End*– David*, Peter
· *Marvel Adventures Hulk Vol. 1: Misunderstood Monster** – Benjamin, Paul
· *Ultimate Wolverine VS. Hulk** – Lindelof, David
· *World War Hulk** – Pak, Greg
· *Indestructible Hulk, Vol. 1: Agent of S.H.I.E.L.D.** – Waid, Mark

Hunger Games: Trilogy (Hunger Games, Catching Fire, Mocking Jay)

The Hunger Games are an annual event where one boy and one girl, aged 12–18, are chosen by lottery from twelve districts to fight until there is only one is left as entertainment for the Capital. It is also to remind the other districts of their place in the world.

- *Hunger Games* – Collin, Suzanne
- *Catching Fire* – Collin, Suzanne
- *Mocking Jay* – Collin, Suzanne
- *Battle Royale* – Takami, Koushun
- *Divergent* – Roth, Veronica
- *Giver* – Lowry, Lois
- *Lord of the Flies* – Golding, William
- *The Lottery and Other Stories* – Jackson, Shirley
- *The Maze Runner* (Book 1) – Dasher, James
- *Inhuman* – Falls, Kat
- *Article 5* – Simmons, Kristen

I Am Number Four

Nine aliens fled to Earth in order to survive. Number Four aka John is hiding as a high school student but comes into his powers and it is recorded and put on the internet. And now those John is hiding from are hunting him once again.

- *I Am Number Four* – Lore, Pittacus
- *The of Power of Six* – Lore, Pittacus
- *The Rise of Nine* – Lore, Pittacus

· *The Angel Experiment* – Patterson, James
· *Uglies* – Westfield, Scott

I Know What You Did Last Summer

A group of teens accidentally kill a man and cover it up. Now someone is killing them one by one in revenge.

· *I Know What You Did Last Summer* – Duncan, Lois
· *Fear Street* (series) – Stine, R.L.
· *The Third Eye* – Duncan, Lois
· *Killing Mr. Griffin* – Duncan, Lois
· *Lovely Bones* – Sebold, Alice
· *Pretty Little Liars* (series) – Shepard, Sara

I Love You, Beth Cooper

The geekiest guy in school proclaims his love to the hottest girl in school during his valedictorian speech. Only to have her show up at his house to show him how the "cool" kids have a goodtime.

· *I Love You, Beth Cooper* – Doyle, Larry
· *Perks of Being a Wallflower* – Chbosky, Stephen
· Ghost World* - Clowes, Daniel
· King Dork – Portman, Frank
· The Astonishing Adventures of Fanboy and Goth Girl – Lyga, Barry
· Nick & Norah's Infinite Playlist – Cohn, Rachel
· *The Summer I Became a Nerd* – Miller, Leah Rae

Indian Jones (*Raiders of the Lost Ark, Temple of Doom, Last Crusade, Kingdom of the Crystal Skull*)

Professor Indian Jones searches the world over to protect ancient artifacts from private collectors to Nazies and everything else in between. At his side are his trusted bull whip and pistol.

- *The Indiana Jones Handbook* – Kiernan, Denise
- *Indiana Jones* (novels) – McCoym Max
- *Indiana Jones Omnibus, Vol.1** – Loeb-Messner, William
- *Indiana Jones and the Raiders of the Lost Ark* – Black, Campbell
- *Indiana Jones and the Last Crusade* – Macgregor, Rob
- *Uncharted: The Fourth Labyrinth* – Golden, Christopher
- *Tomb Raider, Vol. 2: Mystic Artifacts* – Jurgens, Dan

Inkheart

One night, Meggie's father reads aloud from the INKHEART, and Capricorn, an evil ruler escapes from the book and into their living room. Now it is up to Meggie to save the day and stop the Capricorn at all cost and return him to the book in which he has escaped.

- Inkheart – Funke, Cornelia
- Inkspell – Funke, Cornelia
- Inkdeath – Funke, Cornelia
- *Spiderwick Chronicles* – DiTerlizzi, Tony
- *The Neverending Story* – Ende, Michael
- *Return to Labyrinth Vol. 1** - Forbes, Jake

The Invention of Hugo Cabret aka *Hugo*

Hugo is an orphan who lives in a Paris train station, trying to survive in a world which sees him only as a menace. There is a mystery left behind by his father for Hugo to solve which involves a key, a drawing, a notebook and a mechanical mechanized man.

· *The New Way Things Work* – Macaulay, David
· *The Invention of Hugo Cabret* – Selznick, Brian
· *The Adventures of Pinocchio* – Collodi, Carlo & Various
· *Neverwhere* – Gaiman, Neil
· *Wonderstruck* – Selznick, Brian
· *The Tale of Despereaux* – DiCamillo, Kate
· *The Mysterious Benedict Society* – Stewart, Trenton Lee

Iron Man (series)

Billionaire weapons dealer Tony Stark's life is changed when he is attacked and a piece of shrapnel is embedded in his chest near his heart. He is taken captive to create a new weapon for terrorists. With the help of a fellow captive the two create a way to save Stark's life and the first Iron Man armor.

· *Civil War** – Millar, Mark
· *Invincible Iron Man, Vol.1* (Marvel Masterworks)* – Lee, Stan
· *Invincible Iron Man, Vol. 4: Star Disassembled** – Fraction, Matt
· *Iron Man: Armor Wars** – Micheline, David

- *Iron Man: Demon in a Bottle** – Micheline, David
- *Secret Invasion** – Bendis, Brian Michael
- *Iron Man Extremis** – Ellis, Warren
- *Iron Man: Extremis Prose Novel* – Javins, Marie
- *Iron Man, Vol. 1: Believe** – Gillen, Kieron
- *Iron Man: Season One** – Chaykin, Howard
- *Iron Man* – David, Peter

Jack the Giant Slayer

An ancient war between men and giants is reignited when a young farmhand opens a gateway between our world and theirs with so magic beans and a giant bean stalk. It is now up to Jack to save the day and defeat the giants and save the kingdom.

- *The Hobbit* – Tolkien, J.R.R.
- *Jack the Giant Killer* – Various
- *Jack and the Beanstalk* – Various
- *Harry Potter and the Sorcerer's Stone* – Rowling, J.K.
- *A Wizard of Earthsea* – Le Guin, Ursula

James Bond

A British secret with a 00 allowing him to do whatever it takes to keep Queen and County safe no matter what or where the threat comes from.

- *Casino Royale* – Fleming, Ian
- *Doctor No* – Fleming, Ian

- *Goldfinger* – Fleming, Ian
- *Point Break* – Horowitz, Anthony
- *Point Break: The Graphic Novel** – Horowitz, Anthony
- *Skeleton Key* – Horowitz, Anthony
- *Eagle Strike* – Horowitz, Anthony
- *Stormbreaker* – Horowitz, Anthony
- *Stormbreaker: The Graphic Novel**– Johnston, Antony
- *The Young Bond Series, Book One: SilverFin* – Higson, Charlie
- *The Young Bond Series, Book Two: Blood Fever* – Higson, Charlie
- *The Young Bond Series, Book There: Double or Die* – Higson, Charlie

Jaws

A larger than normal great white shark decides to make the beaches off of Amity Island its new buff. And it is up to the local sheriff, a marine biologist and crazy ship captain to take care of this shark. One of the greatest 4th of July movies ever made.

- *Jaws* – Benchley, Peter
- *Congo* – Crichton, Michael
- *Jurassic Park* – **Crichton**, Michael
- *The Devil's Teeth: A True Story of Obsession and Survival Among America's Great White Sharks* – Casey, Susan
- *Prey* – Crichton, Michael
- *Relic* – Preston, Douglas

Jurassic Park Saga (Jurassic Park, The Lost World, Jurassic Park III)

Dinosaurs are brought back to life and chaos ensues in the modern world. Dinosaurs lived. Dinosaurs died. Man comes along. Man brings Dinosaurs back. Dinosaurs eat Man.

- *Dinotopia–* Gurney, James
- *Dinotopia: The World Beneath* – Gurney, James
- *Jurassic Park–* Crichton, Michael
- *The Lost World* – Crichton, Michael
- *The Lost World* – Doyle, Arthur Conan
- *Raptor Red* – Bakker, Robert
- *The Land that Time Forgot* – Burroughs, Edgar Rice

Juno

A girl gets pregnant and decides to give the baby up for adoption to a pair she discovers in the classifieds. Very funny, very witty this is not your typical girl gets pregnant and gives baby up for adoption story.

- *The First Part Last* – Johnson, Angela
- *Juliet, Naked* – Hornby, Nick
- *Nick and Norah's Infinite Playlist* – Cohn, Rachel & Levithan, David
- *Slam* – Hornby, Nick
- *Someone Like You* – Dessen, Sarah
- *A Swift Pure Cry* – Dowd, Siobhan

Kick- Ass/Kick-Ass 2

A kid in the real world wants to be a superhero, but he quickly learns the real life consequences of such actions. And his exploits soon catch the eye of other would be superheroes that are much more violent and better trained to take on the underworld of the city.

· *Fantasy Freaks and Gaming Geeks* – Gilsdorf, Ethan
· *Flyboy Action Figure Comes with Gasmask* – Munroe, Jim
· *Invincible (Book 1): Family Matters* – Kirkman, Robert
· *Kick– Ass** – Millar, Mark
· *Scott Pilgrim, Vol.1 – Scott Pilgrim's Precious Little Life** – O'Malley, Bryan Lee
· *Superior** – Millar, Mike
· *Chasing Shadows* – Avasthi, Swati

The Last Air Bender

Ang, the Last Air Bender and current Avatar, is revived from his ice tomb by a brother and sister. It is now up to them to untie the kingdoms and defeat the tyranny of the Fire Kingdom for good. This can be used for the TV show as well.

· *Bridge of Birds: A Novel of Ancient China That Never Was* – Hughart, Barry
· *Chinese Fairy Tales & Fantasies* – Roberts, Moss
· *Dragon Ball Z Vol.1** – Toriyama, Akira
· *Naruto Vol. 1** – Kishimoto, Masashi

· *Returning My Sister's Face: And Other Far Eastern Tales of Whimsy and Malice* – Foster, Eugie
· *The Remarkable Journey of Prince Jen* – Alexander, Lloyd
· *Romance of the Three Kingdoms Vol. 1* – Kuan– Chung, Lo
· *Romance of the Three Kingdoms Vol. 2* – Kuan– Chung, Lo

Les Miserables

Les Misérables is the story of ex-convict, Jean Valjean (known by his prison number, 24601), who becomes a force for good in the world, but cannot escape his dark past.

· *Les Miserables* – Hugo, Victor
· *The Count of Monte Cristo* – Dumas, Alexandre
· *The Phantom of the Opera* – Leroux, Gaston
· *Madam Bovary* – Flaubert, Gustave
· *Great Expectations* – Dickens, Charles
· *Cerebus** (series) – Sim, Dave

Life of Pi

Pi Patel knows everything there is to know about animals. Pi and his family emigrate from India to North America with the animals from the family zoo. The ship sinks. Pi finds himself alone in a lifeboat with Richard Parker, a 450-pound Bengal tiger.

· *Life of Pi* – Martel, Yann
· *Jungle Book* – Kipling, Rudyard
· *The Second Jungle Book* – Kipling, Rudyard
· *We Bought a Zoo: The Amazing True Story of a Young Family, a Broken Down Zoo, and the 200 Wild Animals that Changed Their Lives Forever* – Mee, Benjamin
· *Robinson Crusoe* – Defoe, Daniel

The Lone Ranger

Based on the radio show, comic books, and novels this is the story of a law man who put on a mask to tame the Wild West along with his sidekick Tonto.

· *The Lone Ranger* – Rudnick, Elizabeth
· *Lone Ranger Omnibus Volume 1 TP* – Matthews, Brett
· *Indian in the Cupboard* – Banks, Lynne Reid
· *Who Was That Masked Man? The Story of the Lone Ranger* – Rothel, David
· *The Lone Ranger* novels – Striker, Fran
· *Green Hornet: Year One Vol. 1 TP** – Wagner, Matt
· *The Shadow*

Lord of the Rings (*Fellowship of the Ring, The Two Towers, Return of the King*)

The grand epic quest which started in *The Hobbit* concludes here with a fellowship to destroy The One Ring is forged, a man will have to step up and become the King he was destined to become and the forces of good must untie to steadfast again the monstrous forces of evil.

- *Dragons of Autumn Twilight* – Weis, Margaret
- *Ending an Ending* – Birt, Danny
- *Eye of the World (The Wheel of Time, Book 1)* – Jordan, Robert
- *The Hero and the Crown* – McKinley, Robin
- *The Hobbit* – Tolkien, J.R. R.
- *Lord of the Ring Vol.1: Fellowship of the Ring* – Tolkien, J.R.R.
- *Lord of the Ring Vol.2: The Two Towers* – Tolkien, J.R.R.
- *Lord of the Ring Vol.3: Return of the King* – Tolkien, J.R.R.
- *Sword of Shannara* – Brooks, Terry
- *The Name of the Wind: The Kingkiller Chronicle Day 1* – Rothfuss, Patrick
- *The Wise Man's Fear: the Kingkiller Chronicle Day 2* – Rothfuss, Patrick
- *Chronicles of the Necromancer* Series – Martian, Gail Z.

The Lovely Bones

This is the story of the murder of a young girl and her family that seeks closer to her death.

· *Lonely Bones* – Sebold, Alice
· *Graveyard Book* – Gaiman, Neil
· *Body Finder* – Derting, Kimberly
· *Desires of the Dead* – Derting, Kimberly
· *The Last Echo* – Derting, Kimberly
· *I Hunt Killers* – Lyga, Barry
· *Game* – Lyga, Barry
· *Extremities: Stories of Death, Murder and Revenge* – Lubar, David
· *Prep School Confidential* – Taylor, Kara
· *Absent* – Williams, Katie

Matrix Saga (Matrix, Matrix Reloaded, Matrix Revolutions, Animatrix)

What is the real world and what isn't? Is man inside the machine or the machine inside the man or are both going on at once. A small group of human freedom fighters must unite with the chosen one to save humanity from the machines.

· *Ghost In the Shell* Volume 1* – Masamune, Shirow
· *Little Brother* – Doctorow, Cory
· *Neuromancer* – Gibson, William
· *Shade's Children* – Nix, Garth
· *Snow Crash* – Stephenson, Neal

Mission Impossible (series)

Ethan Hawk is an IMF agent who is out to save the world no matter the scale or size of the threat.

· *S.H.I.E.L.D: Architects of Forever* – Hickman, Jonathan
· *S.H.I.E.L.D. by Jim Sternako: The Complete Collection* – Steranko, Jim
· *The Young Bond Series, Book One: SilverFin* – Higson, Charlie
· *Strombreaker* – Horowitz, Anthony
· *The Hunchback Assignments* – Slade, Arthur

The Mortal Instruments: City of Bones

Clary Fray heads out to the Pandemonium Club in New York City, she hardly expects to witness a murder committed by three teenagers covered with strange tattoos and brandishing bizarre weapons. Then the body disappears into thin air. After this event her life is turned upside down and inside out and thrown into a mystery of life and death for her and her family.

· *City of Bone* – Clare, Cassandra
· *City of Ashes* – Clare, Cassandra
· *City of Glass* – Clare, Cassandra
· *City of Fallen Angels* – Clare, Cassandra
· *City of Lost Souls* – Clare, Cassandra
· *Demon Trapper* – Oliver, Jana
· *City of Bones: the Offical Illustrated Guide to the Movie* – O'Connor, Mimi

· *The Katerina Trilogy* – Bridges, Robin
· *Shadowhunters Guide* – O'Connor, Mimi

Nicholas Sparks Movies (*Message in a Bottle, A Walk to Remember, The Notebook, Nights in Rodanthe, Dear John, The Last Song, The Lucky One, Safe Haven*)

Nicholas Sparks' books turned to film.

· Nicholas Sparks Books
· *Suzanne's Diary for Nicholas* – Patterson, James
· *Sam's Letters to Jennifer* – Patterson, James
· *Sunday's at Tiffany's* – Patterson, James
· Books by Richard Paul Evans

The Nightmare Before Christmas

Jack Skelington, King of Halloween Town is bored with Halloween and by chance discovers the portals to the other Holiday Towns and decides to take over Christmas with disastrous results.

· *The Adventures of the Princess and Mr. Whiffle: The Thing Beneath the Bed* – Rothfuss, Patrick
· *Coraline* – Gaiman, Neil
· *Lenore: Noogies** – Dirge, Roman
· *The Nightmare Before Christmas* – Burton, Tim
· *The Melancholy Death of Oyster Boy & Other Stories* – Burton, Tim
· *Graveyard Book* – Gaiman, Neil

· *Emile the Strange: Piece of Mind* – Reger, Rob
· *Gris Grimly's Frankenstein* – Shelley, Mary

Now You See Me

Magic and Crime come together and is always one step ahead of anyone who is trying to figure out the trick before it is pulled off.

· *The Complete Idiot's Guide to Street Magic* – Ogde, Tom
· *Magic for Dummies* – Pogue, David
· *The Perfect Score* – Levithan, David
· *The Bling Ring: How a Gang of Fame-Obsessed Teens Ripped Off Hollywood and Shocked the World* – Sales, Nancy

The Outsiders

This is the story about the price of rebellious youth, which centers on two rival gangs in the early 1960s, and the violent turf wars that escalate and tragically claim young lives.

· *The Outsiders* – Hinton, S.E.
· *Autobiography of My Dead Brother* – Myers, Walter Dean
· *The Battle of Jericho* - Draper, Sharon
· *Lord of the Flies* – Golding, William
· *Battle Royal* – Takami, Koushun
· *Rumble Fish* – Hinton, S.E.

· *Rules of Attraction* – Elkeles, Simone
· *Perfect Chemistry* – Elkeles, Simone
· *Chain Reaction* – Elkeles, Simone

Oz the Great and Powerful

This is the prequel to the Wizard of Oz focusing on the Wizard and origins of the witches of Oz.

· *Wicked* – Maguire, Gregory
· *Son of a Witch* – Maguire, Gregory
· *A Lion Among Men* – Maguire, Gregory
· *Out of Oz* – Maguire, Gregory
· *Wizard of Oz* (series) – Baum, L. Frank

Pacific Rim

Giant Monsters (Kiajus) are trying to destroy the Earth and we take the fight to them with Giant Robots (Jaegers).

· *The Call of Cthulhu and Other Weird Stories* – Lovecraft, H.P.
· *Evangelion*** – Sadamoto, Yoshiyuki
· *Godzilla Volume 1*** – Swierczynski, Duane
· *Godzilla on My Mind: Fifty Years of the King of Monsters* – Tsutsui, William
· *Mobile Suit Gundam*** (series) – Various
· *Pacific Rim: The Official Movie Novelization* – Irvine, Alexander

- *Pacific Rim: Man, Machines, and Monsters* – Cohen, David
- *Evangelion* (series) – Sadamoto, Yoshiyuki

Paranormal Activity (series)

A demon haunts/claims the sisters of a family with a secret history of practicing the dark arts.

- *Poltergeists* – Kallen, Stuart A.
- *Ghost Hunters* – Lace, William W.
- *Ghosts* – Parks, Peggy J.
- *Odd Thomas* – Koontz, Daniel
- *The Shining* – King, Stephen
- Books by Christopher Pike
- *The Demonata* (series) – Shan, Darren

Percy Jackson: the Lighting Thief/Sea of Monsters

Zeus's thunderbolt is stolen and Percy discovers he is a demigod, his father Poseidon. It falls to Percy to discover the location of the thunderbolt and who the real thief is.

- *Mythology* – Hamilton, Edith
- *Percy Jackson the Olympians Vol.1: the Lightning Thief* – Riordan, Rick
- *Percy Jackson the Olympians Vol.1: the Lightning Thief: The Graphic Novel** – Riordan, Rick
- *Percy Jackson the Olympians Vol.2: the Sea of Monsters* – Riordan, Rick

- *Percy Jackson the Olympians Vol.3: the Titan's Curse*– Riordan, Rick
- *Percy Jackson the Olympians Vol.4: the Battle of the Labyrinth* – Riordan, Rick
- *Percy Jackson the Olympians Vol.5: The Last Olympian* – Riordan, Rick
- *The Heroes of Olympus, book 1* – Riordan, Rick
- *The Red Pyramid* – Riordan, Rick
- *All Our Pretty Songs,* No. 1 – McCarry, Sarah

Perks of Being a Wallflower

This is the perspective of being the person who is just outside looking in, while dealing with all the firsts of being in high school from dates to kisses and everything in between.

- *Perks of Being a Wallflower* – Chbosky, Stephen
- *Nick and Nora's Infinite Play List* – Cohn, Rachel
- *Scott Pilgrim Color Hardcover Vol. 1** – O'Malley, Brian Lee
- *Fat Angie* – Charlton-Trujillo, E.E.
- *Putting Makeup on the Fat Boy* – Wright, Bill
- *Invisible* – Bates, Marni
- *Since You Asked* – Goo, Maurene
- *Surviving High School* (series) – Doty, M
- *The Summer I Became a Nerd* – Miller, Leah Rae

Pirates of the Caribbean Saga (*The Curse of the Black Pearl, Dead Man's Chest, At World's End, On Stranger Tides*)

Pirates, Pirates and more Pirates; in this tale for the search for the treasure of Davy Jones and a way to save the pirates way of life from both supernatural threats and the British Navy.

- *Bloody Jack* – Meyer, L.A.
- *Capt. Hook: The Adventures of a Notorious Youth* – Hart, J.V.
- *Castaways of the Flying Dutchman* – Jacques, Brian
- *Mad Kestrel* – Massey, Misty
- *Peter and the Starcatchers* – Barry, Dave
- *Pirates!* – Rees, Celia
- *Pirates of the Caribbean: The Price of Freedom* – Crispin, A.C.
- *The Princess Bride* – Goldman, William
- *One Piece Vol.1** – Oda, Eiichiro
- *Stardust* – Gaiman, Neil
- *Treasure Island* – Stevenson, Robert Louis
- *Vampiratres* (series) – Somper, Justin
- *Bloody Jack Adventures* – Meyer, L.A.

Precious

Precious is a girl with the whole world coming crashing down on her, but carries on. She is pregnant once again, by her mother's boyfriend, she has been thrown out of school and must attend a special girl, she eats to feel better and she finds out she has AIDs.

- Bulford Series, Various
- *Drama High: Frenemies* – Divine, L.
- *Like Sisters on the Homefront* – Williams– Garcia, Rita
- *Lost and Found* – Schraff, Anne
- *No Wawsqkhlvy Out* – Langan, Paul
- *Pretty Ugly* – Folan, Karyn
- *Schooled* – Langan, Paul
- *Tyrell – Booth, Coe*

Predator

Aliens use humans as a prey in their hunting safari. It usually involves a rite of passage into adult hood for the alien.

- *Big Game* – Schofield, Sandy
- *Concrete Jungle* – Archer, Nathan
- *Predator: Cold War* – Archer, Nathan
- *Predator Omnibus Vol.1** – Verheiden, Mark
- *Predator Omnibus Vol.2**– Arcudi, John
- *Predator Omnibus Vol.3**– Various
- *Predator: South China Sea* – VanderMeer, Jeff
- *Predator: Turnabout* – Perry, Steve

The Princess Bride

This is the story of a boy, a girl, and their love story; along with a mixture of pirates, sword fights, and miracles.

· *The Princess Bride* – Goldman, William
· *The Black Cauldron* (The Chronicles of Prydain) – Alexander Lloyd
· *Bone** (series) – Smith, Jeff
· *The Hero and the Crown* – McKinley, Robin
· *The Hobbit* – Tolkein, J.R.R.
· *The Last Unicorn* – Beagle, Peter S.
· *Neverending Story* – Ende, Michael
· *Neverwhere* – Gaiman, Neil
· *Stardust* – Gaiman, Neil

The Princess Diaries

Mia Thermopolis is a teenager who discovers she is the heir to the throne of the Kingdom of Genovia, ruled by her grandmother Queen Dowager Clarisse Renaldi. Mia must now learn how to be a princess.

· *The Princess Diaries* – Cabot, Meg
· *Princess in the Spotlight* – Cabot, Meg
· *Princess in Love* – Cabot, Meg
· *Princess in Waiting* – Cabot, Meg
· *Princess in Pink* – Cabot, Meg
· *Princess in Training* – Cabot, Meg
· *Party Princess* – Cabot, Meg
· *Princess on the Brink* – Cabot, Meg

- *Princess Mia* – Cabot, Meg
- *Forever Princess* – Cabot, Meg
- Books by Meg Cabot
- *Pygmalion* – Shaw, George Bernard
- *Just Ella* – Haddix, Margaret
- *Ella Enchanted* – Levine, Gail
- *Sisterhood of the Traveling Pants* – Brashares, Ann
- *Invisible* – Bates, Marni
- *Awkward* – Bates, Marni

Rise of the Guardians

The Guardians of the Holidays and other Supernatural entities my join forces to save the world. The concept behind the characters come from some of the older legends and myths and not their contemporary counterparts.

- *Nicholas St. North and the Battle of the Nightmare King* – Joyce, William
- *E. Aster Bunnymund and the and the Warrior Eggs at the Earth's Core!* – Joyce, William
- *Toothiana, Queen of the Tooth Fairy Armies* – Joyce, William
- *The Art of Rise of the Guardians* – Zahed, Ramin

Robert Langdon (*Angels and Demons, Da Vinci Code*)

The Robert Langdon movies are based on a modern day Indian Jones type character as he solves murders based around archaic symbols found in paintings, money, old manuscripts, Washington DC, and everyday life with a secret society or two thrown in for good measure.

· *Angels and Demons* – Brown, Dan
· *Clockwork Angel* – *Clare*, Cassandra
· *Da Vinci Code* – Brown, Dan
· *The Divine Comedy* – Alighieri, Dante
· *Harry Potter and the Order of the Phoenix* – Rowling, J.K.
· *Holy Blood, Holy Grail* – Baigent, Michael
· Inferno – Brown, Dan
· *The Inferno* - Alighieri, Dante
· *The Lost Symbol* – Brown, Dan
· *Secret Society* – Dolby, Tom
· YA Biographies on Leonardo da Vinci

Robin Hood (various incarnations)

Robin Hood robbed from the rich and gave to the poor. Was he real or just a legend? We may never know the truth, but his legend endures to present day.

· *The Adventures of Robin Hood* – Green, Roger Lancelyn
· *Merry Adventures of Robin Hood* – Pyle, Howard
· *Outlaws of Sherwood* – McKinley, Robin
· *Robin Hood* – Coe, David
· *Robin Hood* – *Holt*, James
· *Robin Hood* – *Gilbert*, Henry
· *Rowan Hood: Outlaw Girl of Sherwood Forest* – Springer, Nancy

Scott Pilgrim VS the World

Boy dreams of girl. Girl turns out to be real. Boy dates girl only to have to defeat her seven evil– exs in order for them to be together. Plus there is rock and roll and battle of the bands thrown into the mix for good measure.

· *Hopeless Savages** – Van Meter, Jen
· *Nick and Norah's Infinite Playlist* – Cohn, Rachel & Levithan, David
· *Scott Pilgrim's Precious Little Life (Vol.1)** – O'Malley, Bryan Lee
· *Scott Pilgrim vs. The World (Vol.2)** – O'Malley, Bryan Lee
· *Scott Pilgrim & the Infinite Sadness (Vol.3)** – O'Malley, Bryan Lee
· *Scott Pilgrim Gets it Together (Vol.4)** – O'Malley, Bryan Lee
· *Scott Pilgrim vs. The Universe (Vol.5)** – O'Malley, Bryan Lee
· *Scott Pilgrim's Finest Hour (Vol.6)** – O'Malley, Bryan Lee
· *The Theory of Everything* – Luna, Kari
· *Dying to Go Viral* – McNicoll, Sylvia
· *The Summer I Became a Nerd* – Miller, Leah Rae

Sex in the City

A modern day woman dealing with life and love in New York City. Her misadventures are shared with her three best friends.

- *All- American Girl* – Cabot Megan
- *The Clique* – Harrison, Lisi
- *Gossip Girl* – *von* Ziegesar, Cecily
- *Little Women* – Alcott, Louisa
- *The Lullaby* – Dessen, Sarah
- *Pride (Seven Deadly Sins)* – Wasserman, Robin
- *Pride and Prejudice* – Austen, Pride
- *Second Helpings* – McCafferty, Megan
- *Sex in the City* – Bushnell, Candace
- *Sisterhood of the Traveling Pants* – Brashares, Ann

Sisterhood of the Traveling Pants

Four friends must part each summer, but they share their summer adventures through a pair of blue jeans.

- *Sisterhood of the Traveling Pants* – Brashares, Ann
- *Second Summer of the Sisterhood* – Brashares, Ann
- *Girls in Pants* – Brashares, Ann
- *Forever in Blue* – Brashares, Ann
- *3 Willows: the Sisterhood Grows* – Brashares, Ann
- *The Truth About Forever* – Dessen, Sarah
- *How My Summer Went Up in Flames* – Dokorski, Salvato

Shrek

Fairy Tales are meshed together and rearranged to tell a brand new tale in Far Far Away Land. This time around the hero is an Ogre, the beautiful princess is transformed into an Ogre to live happily ever after, and a donkey and dragon find love with each other.

· *American Gods* – Gaiman, Neil
· *Beauty: A Retelling of the Story of Beauty and the Beast* – McKinley, Robin
· *Confessions of an Ugly Stepsister* – Maguire, Gregory
· *Fables Vol.1: Legends in Exile* – Willingham, Bill
· *Peter and the Starcatchers* – Barry, Dave
· *Rapunzel's Revenge* – Hale, Shannon
·*Twisted Fairy Tales* – McHugh, Maura
· *Wicked: The Life and Times of the Wicked Witch of the West* – Maguire, Gregory

Spider-Man (series)

Young Peter Parker is bit by a radioactive spider and becomes Spider- Man and learned the lesson of with great power, comes with great responsibility, when he fails to stop a robbery, because he thought himself better. The robber ends up killing Peter's uncle Ben, changing the course of Peter's life forever. This is also good for any number of the Spider-Men cartoons on television.

· *Amazing Spider-Man Vol.1** – *Lee*, Stan
· *The Amazing Spider-Man Vol.2** – Lee, Stan

- *The Amazing Spider-Man: Ultimate Collection, Book 1**
— Straczynski, J. Michael
- *Spider-Man: Kraven's Last Hunt** — DeMatteis, J.M.
- *Ultimate Comics Spider-Man, Vol.1: The World According to Peter Parker** — Bendis, Brian Michael
- *Ultimate Spider-Man: Ultimate Collection, Vol. 1** — Bendis, Brian Michael
- *Spider-Man: The Darkest Hour* — Butcher, Jim
- *Spider-Men* — Bendis, Brian
- *Marvels* — Busiek, Kurt
- *Spider-Man: Death of the Stacys* — Lee, Stan
- *Spider-Man: Blue* — Loeb, Jeph

Star Trek (Original Films, *Star Trek, Star Trek into the Dark*)

To boldly go where no one has gone before; this is a picturesque future where all of humanity has come together to explore the farthest reaches of outer space and coming together with other alien races to form a federation, while dealing with alien threats to the Federation.

- *Blind Man's Bluff* — David, Peter
- *Ender's Game* — Card, Orson Scott
- *Martin Chronicles* — Bradbury, Ray
- *Starclimber* — Oppel, Kenneth
- *Star Trek: Khan — Ruling in Hell ** — Tipton, Scott
- *Star Trek: The Next Generation: Indistinguishable from Magic* — McIntee, David
- *Star Trek: The Original Series: Troublesome Minds* — Galanter, Dave

Star Wars (A New Hope, The Empire Strikes Back, Return of the Jedi, The Phantom Menace, The Clone Wars, Revenge of the Sith)

Star Wars is the classic conflict of good vs. evil, but in outer space with a young hero discovering his potential and rising up to the occasion to save the galaxy. Lightsabers, blasters, space ships, Jedi Knights, and more; Star Wars has become engrained into the culture.

· *Broken (Star Wars: Legacy, Vol.1)** – Ostrander, John
· *Heir to the Empire (Star Wars: The Thrawn Trilogy, Vol.1)* – Zahn, Timothy
· *I, Jedi* – Stackpole, Michael
· *Outcast (Star Wars: Fate of the Jedi, Book 1)* – Allston, Aaron
· *Star Wars: Dark Empire Trilogy HC** – Veitch, Tom
· *Star Wars: The Force Unleashed* – Williams, Sean
· *Star Wars Trilogy* – Lucas, George
· *Vector Prime (Star Wars: The New Jedi Order, Book 1)* – Salvatore, R.A.

Step Up Series (Step Up, Step Up 2, Step Up 3D , Revolution)

The Step Up series focuses on a group of teens and their street dance team as they battle it out with rivals to be the best dance team out there.

· *Come a Stanger* – Voigt, Cynthia
· *Glee: The Beginning: An Original Novel* – Lowell, Sophia

· *Raven* – Diepen, Allison
· *Ten Cents a Dance* – Fletcher, Christine

Superman (*Superman I-4, Superman Returns, Man of Steel*)

It's a bird, it's a plane, it's Superman. Superman was the world's first superhero. Originally the sole survivor of the planet of Krypton, baby Kal El was found by the Kents. He is man/alien that believes in the truth, justice and the American way; the ultimate boy scout.

· *All Star Superman, Vol. 1** – Morrison, Grant
· *The Amazing Adventures of Kavalier & Clay* – Chabon, Michael
· *Kingdom Come** – Waid, Mark
· *The Last Days of Krypton* – Anderson, Kevin
· *Superman: Birthright** – Waid, Mark
· *Superman: Earth One** – Staczynski, J. Michael
· *Superman: Earth One Vol. 2** – Staczynski, J. Michael
· *Superman For All Seasons** – Loeb, Jeph
· *Superman and the Legion of Super– Heroes** – Johns, Geoff
· *Superman: Red Son** – Millar, Mark
· *Superman: Whatever Happened to the Man of Tomorrow?** – Moore, Alan
· *Was Superman a Spy?* – Cronin, Brian

Terminator (Terminator, Terminator 2: Judgment Day, Terminate 3: Rise of the Machines, Terminator Salvation)

Robots from the future return to the past to make sure that they conquer mankind and to make sure mankind can't defeat them.

· *The Eyes of the Killer Robot* – Bellairs, John
· *How to Survive a Robot Uprising* – Wilson, Daniel
· *Skinned (Skinned Trilogy)* – Wasserman, Robin
· *Terminator Omnibus, Vol.1** – Robinson, James
· *Terminator Omnibus, Vol.2** – Various
· *Terminator Salvation: Cold War* – Cox, G.
· *Terminator Salvation: From the Ashes* – Zahn, Timothy
· *Terminator Salvation: Trial by Fire* – Zahn, Timothy
· *I, Robot* – Asimov, Isaac

The Thief Lord

Prosper and Bo, orphaned brothers, have run away to Venice, where a secret community of street urchins exists. Leader of this motley crew of lost children is a boy; who calls himself the Thief Lord.

· *The Thief Lord* – Funke, Cornelia
· *Charlie Bone* (series) – Nimmo, Jenny
· *Oliver Twist* – Dickens, Charles
· *A Bad Beginning* – Snicket, Lemony
· *Harry Potter and the Sorcerer's Stone* – Rowling, J.K.
· *The Invention of Hugo Cabret* – Selznick, Brian

Thor/Thor Dark World

Thor son of Odin is cast from Asgard to learn humility. While on Earth he befriends mortal men, women and other heroes to combat the evils in the world from super villains to gods.

· *The Avengers, Vol. 1* (Marvel Masterworks)* – Lee,
· *D'Aulaires' Book of Norse Myths* – D'Aulaire, Ingri
· *The Mighty Thor, Vol.1 (Marvel Masterworks)** – Lee, Stan
· *The Norse Myths* – Crossley– Holland, Kevin
· *Odd and the Frost Giants* – Gaiman, Neil
· *Thor, Vol.1** – Stracaynski, J. Michael
· *Thor, Vol.1** – Jurgens, Dan
· *Thor, Vol.2** – Stracaynski, J. Michael
· *Thor, Vol.3** – Stracaynski, J. Michael
· *Thor Visionaries – Walter Simonson, Vol.1** – Simonson, Walter

Transformers (*Transformers, Transformers: Rise of the Fallen, Transformers: Dark of the Moon*)

A robotic civil war between the Autobots and Decepticons spills over to Earth where humanity hangs in the balance. These robots are more than meets the eye. This entry is also good for the cartoon show.

· *All Hail Megatron Vol.1 – McCarthy*, Shane
· *I, Robot* – Asimov, Issac
· *Transformers Classics Vol. 1** – Budiansky, Bob

· *Transformers: Generation One Vol. 1* – Sarracini, Chris
· *Transformers: The IDW Collection Vol.1* – Furman, Simon
· *Transformers: Infiltration* – Furman, Simon
· *Transformers Vault: The Complete Transformers Universe – Showcasing Rare Collectibles and Memorabilia* – Hidalgo, Pablo

Twilight Saga (*Twilight, New Moon, Eclipse, Breaking Dawn Pt. 1, Breaking Dawn Pt. 2*)

Girl moves to Alaska. Girl meets Boy. Boy flees Girl, because she smelt too good. Boy turns out to be a vampire who is over 200 years old and still goes to high school. Now thrown in some good vampires, some bad vampires, werewolves and a love triangle and you have the Twilight Saga.

· *The Abused Werewolf Rescue Group* – Jinks, Catherine
· *Blood and Chocolate* – Klause, Annette
· *Blue Bloods (Blue Bloods Book 1)* – de la Cruz, Melissa
· *Breaking Dawn* – Meyer, Stephenie
· *City of Bones* – Clare, Cassandra
· *Dead Until Dark (Southern Vampire Mysteries Vol.1 aka the Sookie Stackhouse Novels)* – Harris, Charlaine
· *Eclipse* – Meyer, Stephenie
· *Eighth Grade Bites (Chronicles of Vladimir Tod, Book 1)* – Brewer, Heather
· *Marked (House of Night Vol.1)* – Cast, P.C.
· *Monster High (Monster High Book)* – Harrison Lisi
· *New Moon* – Meyer, Stephenie

· *The Reformed Vampire Support Group* – Jinks, Catherine
· *Twilight: The Graphic Novel, Vol. 1** – Meyer, Stephenie
· *Twilight*– Meyer, Stephenie
· *Vampire Academy (Vampire Academy Book 1)* – Mead, Richelle
· *Vampire Diaries: The Awakening and the Struggle* – Smith, L.J.
· *Vampire Kisses* – Schreiber, Ellen

The Vampire's Assistant

A mysterious freak show comes to town and young Darren Shan becomes a half-vampire, which might even lead to a greater destiny. First he must leave his past behind him if he is going to survive his new life.

· *Abraham Lincoln: Vampire Hunter* – Grahame– Smith, Seth
· *Cirque du Freak (the Saga of Darren Shan Book 1)* – Shan, Darren
· *Cirque du Freak: the Manga Vol.1**– Shan, Darren
· *Dracula* – Stoker, Bram
· *Eighth Grade Bites (Chronicles of Vladimir Tod, Book 1)* – Brewer, Heather
· *Freaks: Alive, on the Inside!* – Klause, Annette
· *The Vampire's Assistant (the Saga of Darren Shan Book 2)* – Shan, Darren
· *Vampirates: Demons of the Ocean (Book 1)* – Somper, Justin

Warm Bodies

This is a love story like none other. A zombie falls in love a human and something strange begins to happen. This love starts to bring the zombie's humanity and life back to him.

· *Alice in Zombieland* – Showalter, Gena
· *Beautiful Creatures* – Garcia, Kami
· *Rot and Ruin* – Maberry, Jonathan
· *Pride & Prejudice & Zombies* – Austin, Jane
· *Warm Bodies* – Marion, Issac
· *Zom-B* (series) – Shan, Darren

Wizard of Oz

Dorothy of Kansas is transported to the Land of Oz; where she lands on top of a wicked witch, meets a scarecrow without a brain, a tin man without a heart and a lion without courage. All Dorothy wants to do is find a way home and that lies with the Wonderful Wizard of Oz. Oh and the wicked witch Dorothy landed on has a sister who wants revenge and the ruby slippers Dorothy wears. Marvel Comics is currently doing a wonder comic book version of the original Frank Baum books.

· *The Wonderful Wizard of Oz* – Baum, L. Frank
· *The Marvelous Land of OZ* – Baum, L. Frank
· *Ozma of OZ*– Baum, L. Frank
· *Dorothy and the Wizard in OZ* – Baum, L. Frank
· *The Road to OZ* – Baum, L. Frank
· *The Emerald City of OZ* – Baum, L. Frank
· *The Patchwork Girl of OZ* – Baum, L. Frank

· *Tik-Tok of OZ* – Baum, L. Frank
· *The Scarecrow of OZ* – Baum, L. Frank
· *Rinkitink of OZ* – Baum, L. Frank
· *The Lost Princess of OZ* – Baum, L. Frank
· *The Tin Woodman of OZ* – Baum, L. Frank
· *The Magic of OZ* – Baum, L. Frank
· *Glinda of OZ* – Baum, L. Frank
· *Wicked: The Life and Times of the Wicked Witch of the West* – Maguire, Gregory

Wolverine (*X-Men Origins: Wolverine, The Wolverine*)

These are the stories of the X-Men's Wolverine from an exploration of his origins to new adventures.

· *Wolverine** – Claremont, Chris
· *Wolverine: Origins** – Jenkins, Paul
· *Wolverine: Weapon X** – Windsor-Smith, Barry
· *Wolverine: Old Man Logan** – Millar, Mark
· *Wolverine: Inside the World of the Living Weapon* – Manning, Matthew
· *Wolverine: Meltdown* – Simonson, Walter
· *Ultimate Wolverine vs. Hulk* – Lindelof, Damon
· *Wolverine & the X-Men Vol. 1* - Aaron, Jason

World War Z

This is the story of one man's quest to solve the world's zombie problem. His quest takes him all around the world looking for answers to what started the zombie apocalypse and trying to find a way to stop it. It only shares a name with the book.

· *World War Z: An Oral History of the Zombie War* – Brooks, Max
· *The Zombie Survival Guide: Complete Protection from the Living Dead* – Brooks, Max
· *Rot and Ruin* – Mayberry, Jonathan
· *Rotters* – Kraus, Daniel
· *Warm Bodies* – Marion, Issac
· *Zom-B* (series) – Shan, Darren

Wreck-It Ralph

Video game characters come to life as Ralph the villainous star of *Wreck-It Ralph* is no longer happy just playing the part of the villain and wants more out of life; he wants to be the hero.

· *Guinness Book of World Records: Video Game Edition*
· *The Art of Wreck-It Ralph* – Malone, Maggie
· *Scott Pilgrim Color Hardcover Vol. 1** – O'Malley, Brian Lee
· *The Ultimate History of Video Games: From Pong to Pokemon--The Story Behind the Craze That Touched Our Lives and Changed the World* – Kent, Steven
· *The Art of Video Games: From Pac-Man to Mass Effect* – Melissinos, Chris
· *Pokemon Adventures* (series)* – Various
· *Kingdom Heart* (series)* – Amano, Shiro
· *Replay: The History of Video Games* – Donovan, Tristan

X-Men (*X-Men, X-Men 2, X-Men: The Last Stand, X-Men First Class*)

Charles Xavier unites super powered teens (mutants) to teach them to use their powers and fit in with the rest of humanity. Though where there is light, there is also dark; in the Charles's old friend Magneto who wants to enslave humanity with his band of evil mutants. This entry also works on any cartoon based on the X-Men.

· *Astonishing X-Men Vol.1: Gifted* – Whedon, Joss
· *The Angel Experiment (Maximum Ride, Book 1)* – Patterson, James
· *The Lake House* – Patterson, James
· *Ultimate X-Men: Ultimate Collection, Vol.1* – Millar, Mike
· *Uglies* – Westfield, Scott
· *The Uncanny X-Men, Vol.1 (Marvel Masterworks)* – Claremont, Chris
· *X-Men, Vol. 1* – Lee, Stan
· *X-Men: The Dark Phoenix Saga* – Claremont, Chris
· *X-Men: Days of Future Past* – Claremont, Chris
· *X-Men: God Loves, Man Kills* – Claremont Chris
· *X-Men: Mutant Genesis (Marvel Premiere Classic)* – Byrne, John
· *X- Men: Mutant Massacre* – Claremont, Chris
· *X-Men: Season One* – Hopeless, Dennis

Zombieland

Zombies have taken over the world and now it is up to humanity to survive like it has never done before. This entry is also good for the Amazon original series.

· *The Boy Who Couldn't Die* – Sleator, William
· *I Am Legend – Matheson*, Richard
· *Pet Cemetery* – King, Stephen
· *Pride and Prejudice and Zombies* – Austen, Jane
· *Richard Matheson's I Am Legend** – Niles, Steve
· *Rotters* – Kraus, Daniel
· *World War Z: An Oral History of the Zombie War* – Brooks, Max
· *The Zombie Survival Guide: Complete Protection from the Living Dead* – Brooks, Max

TV Shows

Where boys tend to give me movies or video games when I ask them what they like, girls tend to give me TV shows. I figure this is because TV shows are more like series books, which is what they tend to like to read. Then again girls, I notice, will read just about anything. Boys it seems are a lot more finicky about what they are willing to read; in my experience.

Whereas movies come and go quickly and it is hard to keep up with what is going to last, you never know what the life span of a TV show will be. TV executives can cancel a show on a whim it seems. I have seen TV shows killed after only two episodes and I think the record is one. So you never can tell when something is going to vanish off the air waves and this can make it tricky using TV shows as a way to figure out what teens might like to read. Then you have to add in the factor of cable channels and their original programming, which leaves way too many TV shows out there.

There have been times that a teen has named a TV show I hadn't heard of, so I would have to jump on the computer really quick to do a bit of research to find something about it. Normally I can find something that matches up to a program I have seen or have knowledge of. The number of movies and video games out there are a lot more manageable than the number of TV shows.

But never be afraid to ask for another TV show or to look it up online and get a series summary. It helps a lot. IMDB is your friend for both dealing with movies and TV shows. The internet is your friend when it comes to pop culture.

24

Jack Bauer defends the United States from Domestic Terrorism and all of his adventures happening in the window of 24 hours.

· *24 Declassified: Trinity* – Whitman, John
· *24 Declassified: Collateral Damage* – Goldman, Michael
· *24 Declassified: Trojan Horse* – Cerasini, Marc
· *The Mediterranean Caper: A Dirk Pitt Novel* – Cussler, Clive
· *Stormbreaker* – Horowitz, Anthony
· *The Young Bond Series, Book One: SilverFin* – Higson, Charlie

30 Rock

The comedic misadventures of a late night TV show. The show is very much based around the back stage scenes of *Saturday Night Live.*

· *Born Standing Up: A Comic's Life* – Martin, Steve
· *Bossypants* – Fey Tina
· *High Fidelity* – Hornby, Nick
· *Live From New York: An Uncensored History of Saturday Night Live, as Told By Its Stars, Writers and Guests* – Shales, Tom
· *The Secret Diary of Adrian Mole, Aged 13 ¾* – Townsend, Sue

Adventure Time

This is a story of a boy and his dog in the land of Ooo. And that is only the tip of the ice of the insanity, which is *Adventure Time*. Finn is a human boy and Jake the Dog (who can alter his body anyway he likes) his adoptive brother have insane, mystical, and wonderful adventures joined in by Princess Bubble Gum, Marceline the Vampire Queen and Beemo.

· *The Adventure Time Encyclopaedia (Encyclopedia): Inhabitants, Lore, Spells, and Ancient Crypt Warnings of the Land of Ooo Circa 19.56 B.G.E. - 501 A.G.E* – Olson, Martin
· *Adventure Time Vol. 1** - North, Ryan
· *Adventure Time Vol. 1 Playing With Fire** – Corsetto, Danielle
· *Adventure Time: Fionna & Cake** – Allegri. Natasha
· *Adventure Time: Marceline & The Scream Queens** – Gran, Meredith
· *Vic and Blood* – Ellison, Harlan
· *Dragons of Autumn Twilight* (Dragonlance Chronicles, Vol. 1) – Weis, Margaret

Agents of S.H.E.I.L.D.

Supreme Headquarters, International Espionage, Law-Enforcement Division or Strategic Hazard Intervention Espionage Logistics Directorate or Strategic Homeland Intervention, Enforcement and Logistics Division they are all S.H.E.I.L.D. and they are an ever present eye protecting the Marvel Universe.

· *S.H.I.E.L.D.: Architects of Forever** – Hickman, Jonathan
· *S.H.I.E.L.D. by Jim Steranko: The Complete Collection** – Steranko, Jim
· *Indestructible Hulk, Vol. 1: Agent of S.H.I.E.L.D.** – Waid, Mark
· *S.H.I.E.L.D.: Nick Fury VS. S.H.I.E.L.D.** – Harras, Bob
· *Secret War** - Bendis, Brian
· *Secret Warriors, Vol. 1: Nick Fury, Agent of Nothing* – Bendis, Brian
· *Wolverine & Nick Fury: Scorpio* – Goodwin, Archie
· *Strombreaker* (Alex Rider Series) –
· *Hunchback Assignments*
· *Young James Bond series*

American Idol

Singing contestants from all over the United States compete to be the next American Idol. Each contestant sing and compete for the votes of the American viewing audience.

· *American Idol: Celebrating 10 Years* – Halperin, Shirley
· *American Idol: The Untold Story* – Rushfield, Richard

· *Carrie Underwood* (A Blue Banner Biography) – Tracy, Kathleen
· *Kelly Clarkson* (A Blue Banner Biography) – Tracy, Kathleen
· *I Don't Mean to Be Rude, But...: Backstage Gossip from American Idol & the Secrets that Can Make You a Star* – Cowell, Simon
· *Chris Daughtry* (A Blue Banner Biography) – Tracy, Kathleen

Arrow

Oliver Queen was spoiled rich and didn't care who he hurt living a lifestyle of excess. Until the day the boat he was on with his father exploded and he learned the truth about the city in which he lived in; along with the darkside of his family. Oliver had to learn to live and survive on *the island*. Now he has returned home and is going to save the city from those who want to destroy it. Arrow is loosely based off of DC Comics Green Arrow.

· *Arrow Vol. 1* – Guggenheim, Marc
· *Green Arrow: The Longbow Hunter* – Grell, Mike
· *Green Arrow Vol. 1: Hunters Moon* – Grell, Mike
· *Green Lantern/Green Arrow* – Adams, Neal
· *Green Lantern/Green Arrow Collection - Vol. 2* – O'Neil, Dennis
· *The Merry Adventures of Robin Hood* – Pyle, Howard
· *Robinson Crusoe* – Defoe, Daniel

Bates Motel

The story of young Norman Bates and how he became the killer we see him in the classic Alfred Hitchcock movie Psycho, which is based loosely on serial killer Ed Gein.

· *Psycho A Novel* – Bloch, Robert
· *Deviant: The Shocking True Story of Ed Gein, the Original Psycho* – Schechter, Harold
· *Lovely Bones* – Sebold, Alice
· *Whoever Fights Monsters: My Twenty Years Tracking Serial Killers for the FBI* – Ressler, Robert
· *Darkly Dreaming Dexter* (*Dexter* Series) – Lindsay, Jeff

Big Bang Theory

This is a show about four stereotypical geeks, their hot female next door neighbor and their misadventures of life and love. The show has it all from comic books, video games, pop culture and more.

· *The Astonishing Adventures of Fanboy and Goth Girl* – Lyga, Barry
· *DORK TOWER V Understanding Gamers** – Kovalic, John
· *Fantasy Freaks and Gaming Geeks* – Gilsdorf, Ethan
· *Geektastic: Stories From the Nerd Herd* – Black, Holly
· *Into the Wild Nerd Yonder* – Halpern, Julie
· *Just a Geek* – Wheaton, Wil
· *The Summer I Became a Nerd* – Miller, Leah Rae
· The Way Science Works – Kerrod, Robin

Big Time Rush

This show focuses on the Hollywood misadventures of four hockey players from Minnesota after they are selected to form a boy band.

· *Big Time Rush* Books – Golden Books
· *The Cheetah Girls Livin' Large: Books 1 - 4* – Gregory, Deborah
· *'N Sync* – Grabowski, John
· *One Direction: What Makes You Beautiful* – Boone, Mary
· *Teens, TV, and Tunes: The Manufacturing of American Adolescent Culture* – Greene, Doyle

Bleach

Ichigo Kurosaki obtains the powers of a Soul Reaper and now he must defend humanity against evil spirits and guide souls headed to the afterlife. (Anime)

· *Bleach* (series)* – Kubo, Tite
· *Naruto* (series)* – Kishimoto, Mashashi
· *Shaman King* (series)* – Takei, Hiroyuki
· *Soul Eater* (series)* – Ohkubo, Atsushi
· *YuYu Hakusho* (series)* – Togashi, Yoshihiro

Bones

The world of forensic anthropology is used to help solve crimes with the FBI.

· *Deja Dead (Temperance Brennan Novels, book 1)* – Reich, Kathy
· *Death du Jour (Temperance Brennan Novels, book 2)* – Reich, Kathy
· *Deadly Decisions (Temperance Brennan Novels, book 3)* – Reich, Kathy
· *Fatal Voyage (Temperance Brennan Novels, book 4)* – Reich, Kathy
· *Grave Secrets (Temperance Brennan Novels, book 5)* – Reich, Kathy
· *Bare Bones (Temperance Brennan Novels, book 6)* – Reich, Kathy
· *Monday Mourning (Temperance Brennan Novels, book 7)* – Reich, Kathy
· *Cross Bones (Temperance Brennan Novels, book 8)* – Reich, Kathy
· *Break No Bones (Temperance Brennan Novels, book 9)* – Reich, Kathy
·*Bones to Ashes (Temperance Brennan Novels, book 10)* – Reich, Kathy
· *Devil Bones (Temperance Brennan Novels, book 11)* – Reich's Kathy
· *206 Bones (Temperance Brennan Novels, book 12)* – Reich, Kathy
· *Spider Bones (Temperance Brennan Novels, book 13)* – Reich, Kathy
· *Virals* – Reich, Kathy

· *Seizure: A Virals Novel* – Reich, Kathy
· *Code: A Virals Novel* – Reich, Kathy

Burn Notice

A spy who has been cut loose from his agency and now he is trying to find out who burned him and get his revenge. Or at the very least get the burn notice taken off of him, so he can once again live a normal life.

· *Burn Notice:* – Goldberg, Tod
· *Burn Notice: the Giveaway* – Goldberg, Tod
· *Burn Notice: the Reformed* – Goldberg, Tod
· *Quantum of Solace: The Complete James Bond Short Stories* – Fleming Ian
· *Scorpia* – Horowitz, Anthony

The Carrie Diaries

These are the adventures of Carrie from *Sexy in the City* set during her teenage years.

· *The Carrie Diaries* – Bushnell, Candace
· *Sex in the City* – Bushnell, Candace
· *Gossip Girls* (series) – von Ziegesar, Cecily
· *It Girl* (series) – von Ziegesar, Cecily
· *Private Novel* (series) – Brian, Kate
· *The Clique* (series) – Harrison, Lisi

Castle

Richard Castle has lost the inspiration to write until he decides to use his influence to shadow a NYPD Detective and Nikki Heat is born.

- *Frozen Heat* (Nikki Heat) – Castle, Richard
- *Heat Wave* (Nikki Heat) – Castle, Richard
- *Master of Murder* – Pike, Christopher
- *Naked Heat* (Nikki Heat) – Castle, Richard
- *A Northern Light* – Donnelly, Jennifer
- *To Kill A Mockingbird* – Lee, Harper
- *Castle: A Calm Before Storm** – Castle, Richard
- *Castle: Richard Castle's Deadly Storm** – Castle, Richard
- *Castle: Richard Castle's Storm Season** - Bendis, Brian

Chuck

An everyday tech guy working at a big box store accidently downloads into his brain a CIA main frame. Now it is up to CIA operative and military sniper to keep this every day bloke alive, while dealing with threats against national security.

- *Artemis Fowl* (series) – Colfer, Eoin
- *Chuck** – Johnson, Peter
- *Eagle Strike* – Horowitz, Anthony
- *Fledgling: Jason Steed* – Cooper, Mark
- *Perfect Cover* – Barnes, Jennifer
- *Skeleton Key* – Horowitz, Anthony
- *Stormbreaker* – Horowitz, Anthony

Criminal minds

FBI profilers (the BAU) travel around the country solving the crimes of serial murders.

· *Criminal Minds: Killer Profile* – Collins, Max Allan
· *Criminal Minds: Finishing School* – Collins, Max Allan
· *Criminal Minds: Jump Cut* – Collins, Max Allan
· *The Lovely Bones* – Sebold, Alice
· *Sherlock Holmes: The Complete Novels and Stories Vol. 1* – Doyle, Sir Arthur Conan
· *Whoever Fights Monsters: My Twenty Years Tracking Serial Killers for the FBI* – Ressler, Robert
· *Forensics: Uncover the Science and Technology of Crime Scene Investigation* – Mooney, Carla

CSI (CSI, CSI Miami, CSI New York)

Crime Scene Investigation that takes place in Las Vegas, Miami, and New York. These scientists and police officers work to solve crimes, murders and theft.

· *Binding Ties (CSI: Crime Scene Investigation)* – Collins, Max Allan
· *CSI: Crime Scene Investigation: Mortal Wounds* – Collins, Max Allan
· *CSI: Miami: Cut and Run* – Cortez, Donn
· *CSI: Sin City* – Collins, Max Allan
· *Investigating CSI: An Unauthorized Look Inside the Crime Labs of Las Vega, Miami and New York* – Cortez, Donn

· *Sherlock Holmes: The Complete Novels and Stories Vol. 1* – Doyle, Sir Arthur Conan
· *True Stories of CSI: The Real Crimes Behind the Best Episodes of the Popular TV Show* – Ramsland, Katherine
· *Extremities: Stories of Death, Murder and Revenge* – Lubar, David
· *Forensics: Uncover the Science and Technology of Crime Scene Investigation* – Mooney, Carla
· *Criminal* – McVoy, Terra

Desperate House Wives

Chick Lit brought to the small screen. Five house wives living on Wisteria Lane and their insane misadventures from life to love.

· *The Clique (The Clique Book 1)* – Harrison, Lisi
· *Gossip Girls #1: A Novel (Gossip Girl Series)* – von Ziegesar, Cecily
· *The It Girl (It Girl #1)* – con Ziegesar, Cecily
· *Lust (Seven Deadly Sins)* – Wasserman, Robin
· *The Princess Diaries* – Cabot, Meg
· *Private (Private, Book 1)* – Brian, Kate

Destroy, Build Destory

Two Teams of kids destroy things and then rebuild them into a new machine in a competition to destroy what the other team has built.

· *The New Way Things Work* – Macaulay, David
· *The Way Science Works* – Kerrod, Robin
· *Built to Last* – Macaulay, David
· *The Dangerous Book for Boys* – Iggulden, Conn
· *The Boys' Book Of Survival (How To Survive Anything, Anywhere)* – Scholastic

Dexter

Dexter Morgan is a serial killer. He is a serial killer with a code. The code will only let him kill other murders and killers. Dexter works for the police department as a blood splatter expert and crime scene analyst.

· *Artemis Fowl* (series) – Colfer, Eoin
· *Darkly Dreaming Dexter* – Lindsay, Jeff
· *Dearly Devoted Dexter* – Lindsay, Jeff
· *Dexter in the Dark* – Lindsay, Jeff
· *Dexter by Design* – Lindsay, Jeff
· *Dexter is Delicious* – Lindsay, Jeff
· *Double Dexter* – Lindsay, Jeff
· *Whoever Fights Monsters: My Twenty Years Tracking Serial Killers for the FBI* – Ressler, Robert
· *Extremities: Stories of Death, Murder and Revenge* – Lubar, David

· *Forensics: Uncover the Science and Technology of Crime Scene Investigation* – Mooney, Carla

Doctor Who

The Doctor, his companions and the TARDIS travel through space and time with many misadventures; while dealing with a whole cavalcade of villains, space aliens, and time lords trying to stop him along the way. This is the longest running sci-fi series of all time.

A side note Doctor Who novels were originally created because the BBC didn't do reruns of their episodes. So the only way to relive the adventures was through the Target novelizations. Eventually they published original adventures of the Classic Doctors (Doctors 1-8) and now they publish adventures of the NUWho Doctors (9-11).

Originally Doctor Who novels were only printed in the UK and were imported to the US, making it hard to know what was actually in print at any given time. Though just recently the BBC realized the American readership for the Doctor's adventures. So they have begun partnering with a publisher in the states, which has helped make the availability of these novels more stable and without the import price.

· *Doctor Who* Novels – Various
· *Dirk Gently's Holistic Detective Agency* – Adams, Douglas
· *Doctor Who: Coming of the Terraphiles HC* – Moorcock, Michael
· *Doctor Who: The Forgotten** – Lee Tony

· *Doctor Who: The TARDIS Handbook* – Tribe, Steve
· *Douglas Adams's Starship Titanic* – Jones, Terry
· *The Hitchhiker's Guide to the Galaxy* – Adams, Douglas
· *Life, the Universe, and Everything* – Douglas, Adams
· *Neverwhere* – Gaiman, Neil
· *Red Dwarf Omnibus* – Naylor, Grant
· *The Restaurant at the End of the Universe* – Adams, Douglas
· *TimeRiders* (series) – Scarrow, Alex
· *Artemis Fowl* (series) – Colfer, Eoin
· *Doctor Who: Who-olgy* – *Scott, Cavan*
· *Doctor Who: The Vault: Treasures from the First 50 Years* – Hearn, Marcu
· *Doctor Who: Official Annual XXXX* – Various

Downton Abbey

British period television at its best; *Downton Abbey* is set in the Yorkshire country estate of Downton Abbey. The show depicts the lives of the aristocratic Crawley family and their servants in the post-Edwardian era.

· *Lady Almina and the Real Downton Abbey: The Lost Legacy of Highclere Castle* - The Countess of Carnarvon
· *The World of Downton Abbey* – Fellowes, Julian
· *The Chronicles of Downton Abbey* – Fellowes, Julian
· *Little Women* – Alcott, Louisa
· *Emma* – Austen, Jane
· *Wuthering Heights* – Bronte, Emily
· *Pride and Prejudices* – Austin, Jane

Elementary

An American modernization of Sherlock Holms set in New York City. This show is based on original adventures and stories.

· *Sherlock Holmes: The Complete Novels and Stories Vol. 1* – Doyle, Sir Arthur Conan
· *Nancy Drew* (series) – Various
· *Hardy Boys* (series) – Various
· *The Mysterious Benedict Society* (series) – Stewart, Trenton
· *The Science of Sherlock Holmes: From Baskerville Hall to the Valley of Fear, the Real Forensics Behind the Great Detective's Greatest Cases* – Wagner, E.J.
· *Brilliant Deduction: The Story of Real-Life Great Detectives* - Kuhns, Matt
· *Dr. Joe Bell: Model for Sherlock Holmes* – Liebow, Ely M.
· *Black Ice* (*Sherlock Holmes the Legend Begins*) – Lane, Andrew

Falling Skies

The world has been invaded and it is the day after. The aliens want humanity wiped from the planet. Luckily a small group of resistant fighters remain and have slowly brought the fight back to the alien invaders.

· *Ender's Game* (series) – Card, Orson Scott
· *The Host* – Meyer, Stephanie
· *Falling Skies** – Tobin, Paul

· *Falling Skies Volume 2: The Battle of Fitchburg* – Tobin, Paul
· *Starship Troopers* – Heinlein, Robert

Futurama

This is the world of the future as envisioned by the creator of the *Simpsons* Matt Groening.

· *The Simpsons Futrama Crossover Crisis** – Groening, Matt
· *Futurama: The Timer Bender Trilogy** – Groening, Matt
· *Futurama– O– Rama** – Groening, Matt
· *Futurama Conquers the Universe** – Groening, Matt
· *Futurama Adventures** – Groening, Matt
· *World's Fair* – Doctorow, E.L.

Game of Thrones

One of the bloodiest, politically driven fantasy shows on TV. No one is safe and can die at any moment. This is a show you will either love or hate. The show is based on the George R.R. Martin series *A Song of Ice and Fire*.

· *A Game of Thrones* – Martin, George R.R.
· *A Clash of Kings* – Martin, George R.R.
· *A Storm of Swords* – Martin, George R.R.
· *A Feast for Crows* – Martin, George R.R.
· *A Dance with Dragons* – Martin, George R.R.
· *The Winds of Winter* – Martin, George R.R.

- *Wheel of Time* (series) – Jordan, Robert
- *Lord of the Ring* (series) – Tolkien, J.R.R.
- *The Silmarillion* – Tolkien, J.R.R.
- *Shannara* (series) – Brooks, Terry
- *Dragons of Autumn Twilight (Dragonlance Chronicles, Vol.1)* – Weis, Margaret

Glee

Glee club, geeks, jocks, high school, evil cheerleading coach and life are just a part of the world of Glee.

- *Don't Stop Believin': The Unofficial Guide to Glee* – Balser, Erin
- *Glee: The Beginning: An Original Novel* – Lowell, Sophia
- *Glee: Foreign Exchange: An Original Novel* – Lowell, Sophia
- *Glee: Summer Break: An Original Novel* – Lowell, Sophia
- *Lady Gaga: Behind the Fame* – Herbert, Emily
- *Madonna* – Morton, Andrew

Gossip Girl

A TV show based on the besting selling YA chick lit by Cecily von Ziegesar.

- *Gossip Girl (book 1)* – von Ziegesar, Cecily
- *You Know You Love Me (book 2)* – von Ziegesar, Cecily
- *All I Want is Everything (book 3)* – von Ziegesar, Cecily
- *Because I'm Worth (book 4)* – von Ziegesar, Cecily

· *You're the One That I Want (book 5)* – von Ziegesar, Cecily
· *Nobody Does It Better (book 6)* – von Ziegesar, Cecily
· *Nothing Can Keep Us Together (book 7)* – von Ziegesar, Cecily
· *Only in Your Dreams (book 8)* – von Ziegesar, Cecily
· *Would I Lie to You? (book 9)* – von Ziegesar, Cecily
· *Don't You Forget About Me (book 10)* – von Ziegesar, Cecily
· *Gossip Girl: It Had To Be You (book 11)* – von Ziegesar, Cecily
· *I will Always Love You (book 12)* – von Ziegesar, Cecily
· *Gossip Girl: The Carlyles (The Carlyles book 1)* – von Ziegesar, Cecily
· *You Just Can't Get Enough (The Carlyles book 2)* – von Ziegesar, Cecily
· *Take a Chance on Me (The Carlyles book 3)* – von Ziegesar, Cecily
· *Love the One You're With (The Carlyles book 4)* – von Ziegesar, Cecily
· *Rainbow Boys – Sanchez, Alex*

Grimm

All the Grimm fairy tales are true. The lineage, of the family, Grimm hunts the monsters they wrote about keeping the world safe from them.

· *Fables* (series) – Willingham, Bill
· *Grimm - Aunt Marie's Book of Lore* – Titan Books
· *Twisted Fairy Tales* – McHugh, Maura

· *Fairy Tales from the Brothers Grimm* – Pullman, Philip

Hemlock Grove

A supernatural soap opera focusing on two families; one is wealthy, the other are gypsies. But both these families hide horrifying secrets of the supernatural order. This was one of Netflix's original shows.

· *Hemlock Grove* – McGreevy, Brian
· *Blood and Chocolate* – Klause, Annette
· *Luna – Fargo, Gina*
· *Ivy Cole and the Moon – Fargo, Gina*
· *Vampire Kisses* (series) – Schreiber, Ellen
· *Vampire Diaries* (series) – Smith, L.J.
· *Twilight Graphic Novels* (series) – Myers Stephanie
· *Frankenstein* – Shelly, Mary
· *Gris Grimly's Frankenstein – Shelly, Mary*

House

Dr. House is one of the most brilliant doctor's in the world, but he is a jackass. He is more interested in the medical mystery than the person he is helping to heal.

· *Andromeda Strain* – Crichton, Michael
· *Double Helix* – Werlin, Nancy
· *House, M.D.: The Official Guide to the Hit Medical Drama* – Jackman, Ian
· *Outbreak* – Cook, Robin

· *The Secret of the Yellow Death: At True Story of Medical Sleuthing* – Jurmain, Suzanne

How I Met Your Mother

This is the story of five friends living in New York City. Lily and Marshal are married. Robin is trying to further her reporting career. Barney is a womanizer and no one is quite sure what he does for a living. Then there is Ted who is trying to find the love of his life.

· *Angus, Thongs and Full– Frontal Snogging* (*Confessions of Georgia Nicolson*) – Rennison, Louise
· *Ghost World** – Clowes, Daniel
· *I Love You Beth Cooper* – Doyle, Larry
· *Scott Pilgrim's Precious Little Life* – O'Malley, Bryan Lee
· *Sloppy Firsts* – McCafferty, Megan
· *Spanking Shakespeare* – Wizner, Jake

How to Train Your Dragon

This show is based on the hit Dream Works movie *How to Train Your Dragon* (so this entry works for both the film and TV Show).

· *Dragon Riders of Pernn* (series) – McCaffrey, Anne
· *Dragonlance Chronicles* (series) – Weis, Margaret
· *How to Train Your Dragon* (series) – Cowell, Cressida
· *Dragon Rider* – Funke, Cornelia
· *The Pit Dragon Chronicles* – Yolen, Jane

Law and Order (Law & Order, Law & Order Special Victims Unit, Law & Order Criminal Intent, Law & Order UK)

Law and Order is one of the longest running shows/series about crime, law and justice on TV.

- *Bloodhound* – Pierce, Tamora
- *Goldfish** – Bendis, Brian Michael
- *Law & Order: Special Victims Unit: The Unofficial Companion* – Green, Susan
- *Nineteen Minutes* – Picoult, Jodi
- *Powers Vol.1: Who Killed Retro Girl?** – Bendis, Brian Michael
- *The Rag and Bone Shop* – Cormier, Robert
- *To Kill a Mocking Bird – Lee*, Harper
- *Torso** – Bendis, Brian Michael
- *True Stories of Law & Order: The Real Crimes Behind the Best Episodes of the Hit TV Show* – Dwyer, Kevin
- *True Stories of Law & Order: SVU* – Dwyer, Kevin

Legend of Korra

The sequel to *Avatar: The Last Airbender*. It is set in a much more modern/steampunkesq sort of environment in the world of the orient. There is a still lot of martial arts and elemental bending in the story.

- *Endgame* (*Legend of Korra*) – David, Erica
- *Revolution* (*Legend of Korra*) – David, Erica

· *The Legend of Korra: Book 1 – Air, The Art of the Animated Series* – DiMartino, Michael
· *Young Samurai: The Way of the Sword* – Bradford, Chris
· *Young Samurai: The Way of the Dragon* – Bradford, Chris
· *Young Samurai: Way of the Warrior* – Bradford, Chris

My Little Pony Friendship is Magic

Something I don't even understand. Friendship is magic. Bronies. My Little Pony for the modern age.

· *Bone** (series) – Smith, Jeff
·*My Little Pony: The Elements of Harmony: Friendship is Magic: The Official Guidebook* – Snider, Brandon T.
· *My Little Pony Volume 1: Friendship Is Magic** - Cook, Katie
· *My Little Pony Volume 2: Friendship is Magic** – Nuhfer, Heather
· *My Little Pony Mane Tales Volume 1 (My Little Pony - Micro Series)* – Zahler, Thom

Mythbusters

The building put the myths to the test to discover if it is possible or not.

· *Mythbusters Science Fair Book* – Margles, Samantha
· *Mythbusters: Confirm or Bust! Science Fair Book #2* – Margles, Samantha

- *Mythbusters: Don't Try This at Home* – Packard, Mary
- *The Way Science Works* – Kerrod, Robin
- *Mythbusters: The Explosive Truth Behind 30 of the Most Perplexing Urban Legends of All Time* – Zimmerman, Keith
- *Urban Legends* – Stewart, Gail

NCIS

This is the Naval Criminal Investigation Service; they deal with crimes and murder against military personal.

- *Blood Evidence (NCIS Series #2)* – Odem, Mel
- *Blood Lines (NCIS Series #3)* – Odem, Mel
- *The Hunt for Red October* – Clancy, Tom
 Paid in Blood (NCIS Series #1) – Odom, Mel
- *Patriot Games* – Clancy Tom
- *Forensics: Uncover the Science and Technology of Crime Scene Investigation* – Mooney, Carla
- *Criminal* – McVoy, Terra

Once Upon a Time

The show takes place in the seaside town of Storybrooke, Maine, where its residents are actually characters from various fairy tales. They were transported to the "real world" town and robbed of their real memories by a powerful curse.

- *Once Upon a Time: Shadow of the Queen** – Thompson, Dan

- *Fables** (series) – Willingham, Bill
- *Once Upon a Time – Behind the Magic* – Titan Books
- *Reawakened: A Once Upon a Time Tale* – Beane, Odette
- *Fairest, Vol. 1 (Fables)* – Willingham, Bill
- *Between the Lines* – Picoult, Jodi
- *Beauty* – Ohlin, Nancy

One Tree Hill

Another young adult TV drama that started off with showing the main characters in high school and then it jumped ahead to their time after college.

- *Gossip Girl* – von Ziegesar, Cecily
- *Homecoming Queen (Carter House Girls, Book 3)* – Carlson, Melody
- *It Girl* – von Ziegesar, Cecily
- *Inner Circle* – Brian, Kate
- *Mixed Bags (Carter House Girls, Book 1)* – Carlson, Melody
- *One Tree Hill: #1 The Beginning* – Markas, Jenny
- *One Tree Hill: Novelizations #2: A Heart So True* – Lotto, Anna

Power Rangers

Live action anime based of the Japanese show Sentai. Teenagers morph in battle suits to deal with the threat at hand, which always leads to a Monster verses Zord fight.

· *Sailor Moon* (series) -
· *Mobile Suit Gundum* – Various
· *Power Rangers** (Tokyo Pop/Manga) – various
· *Battle of the Planets** (series) – various
· *Voltron Year One TP** - Thomas, Brandon
· *Voltron Vol. 1: The Sixth Pilot* – Thomas, Brandon
· *Voltron Force, Vol. 1: Shelter from the Storm* – Smith, Brian

Pretty Little Lairs

This is the story of four girls whose clique falls apart after the disappearance of their leader in the 8th grade. When the girls are in high school, the missing girl's body is found, and they begin receiving various messages from someone using the alias "A" who threatens to expose their secrets and get revenge on them for what happened to "A".

· *Pretty Little Liars* – Shepard, Sara
· *Flawless* – Shepard, Sara
· *Perfect* – Shepard, Sara
· *Unbelievable* – Shepard, Sara
· *Wicked* – Shepard, Sara
· *Killer* – Shepard, Sara
· *Heartless* – Shepard, Sara
· *Wanted* – Shepard, Sara
· *Twisted* – Shepard, Sara
· *Ruthless*– Shepard, Sara
· *Stunning* – Shepard, Sara
· *Burned* – Shepard, Sara
· *Crushed* – Shepard, Sara

- *Deadly* – Shepard, Sara
- *Pretty Little Secrets* – Shepard, Sara
- *Ali's Pretty Little Lies* – Shepard, Sara
- *I Know What You Did Last Summer* – Duncan, Lois
- *Dangerous Girls* – Haas, Abigail

Reality TV (Jersey Shore, Duck Dynasty, Honey Boo Boo, Survivor, etc.)

Any number of "reality tv" shows. They all have books out there. Some are painfully bad and funny at the same time.

- *Here's the Situation: A Guide to Creeping on Chicks, Avoiding Grenades, and Getting in Your GTL on the Jersey Shore* – Sorrentino, Mike
- *Confessions of a Guidette* – Polizzi, Nicole
- *The Rules According to JWOWW: Shore-Tested Secrets on Landing a Mint Guy, Staying Fresh to Death, and Kicking the Competition to the Curb* – Farley, Jenni
- *How to Honey Boo Boo: The Complete Guide on How to Redneckognize the Honey Boo Boo in You* – Shannon & Thompson Family
- *The Duck Commander Family: How Faith, Family, and Ducks Built a Dynasty* – Robertson, Willie
- *Happy, Happy, Happy: My Life and Legacy as the Duck Commander* – Robertson, Phil
- *My Ox Is Broken!: Roadblocks, Detours, Fast Forwards and Other Great Moments from Tv's 'the Amazing Race'* - Castro, Adam-Troy
- *Reality TV: An Insider's Guide to TV's Hottest Market* – Devolld, Troy

Sherlock

The British take on a modern Sherlock Holmes set in London; brought to you by Stephen Moffat and Mark Gatiss. These are modern retellings of Sherlock Holmes adventures.

· *Sherlock Holmes: The Complete Novels and Stories Vol. 1* – Doyle, Sir Arthur Conan
· *The Sherlock Files: The Official Companion to the Hit Television Series* – Adams, Guy
· *Sherlock: A Study in Scarlet (Sherlock (BBC Books))* – Doyle, Sir Arthu Conan
· *Sherlock: The Casebook* – Adams, Guy
· *The Science of Sherlock Holmes: From Baskerville Hall to the Valley of Fear, the Real Forensics Behind the Great Detective's Greatest Cases* – Wagner, E.J.
· *Brilliant Deduction: The Story of Real-Life Great Detectives* - Kuhns, Matt
· *Dr. Joe Bell: Model for Sherlock Holmes* – Liebow, Ely M.
· *Black Ice* (*Sherlock Holmes the Legend Begins*) – Lane, Andrew

Simpsons

Matt Groening created the longest running animated show in television history. The Simpsons follow the adventures of Homer, Margie, Bart, Lisa and Maggie; along with a whole host of other colorful characters. This show helped pave the way for other primetime animated shows.

· *Bart Simpson's Guide to a Life: A Wee Handbook for the Perplexed* – Groening, Matt
· *Bart Simpson's Treehouse of Horror Heebie– Jeeie Hullabaloo** – Groening, Matt
· *Simpsons Comics Unchained** – Groening, Matt
· *Simpsons Comics Get Some Fancy Book Learnin'** – Groening, Matt
· *The Simpsons One Step Beyond Forever: A complete Guide to Our Favorite Family... Continued Yet Again* – Groening, Matt

Smallville

The small screen version of how Clark Kent became Superman.

· *Superboy: The Boy of Steel** – Johns, Geoff
· *Superman: Earth One** – Staczynski, J. Michael
· *Superman For All Seasons** – Loeb, Jeph
· *Superman: The Man of Steel, Vol.1** – Byrne, John
· *Superman: Secret Origin** – Johns, Geoff

Soul Eater

Death Weapon Meister Academy is where three teams consisting of a weapon meister and a human weapon are trying to make weapon a "death scythe." They must collect the souls of 99 evil humans and one witch if they fail they will have to start all over again.

· *Bleach* (series)* – Kubo, Tite
· *Naruto* (series)* – Kishimoto, Mashashi
· *Shaman King* (series)* – Takei, Hiroyuki
· *Soul Eater* (series)* – Ohkubo, Atsushi
· *YuYu Hakusho* (series)* – Togashi, Yoshihiro

Star Wars the Clone Wars

This is the continuing story of the Clone Wars that occur between Star Wars: *The Clone Wars* and *Revenge of the Sith*.

· *The Cestus Deception (Star Wars: The Clone Wars Novel)* – Barnes, Steven
· *The Clone Wars (Star Wars)* – Traviss, Karen
· *Defenders of the Republic (Star Wars: The Clone Wars)* – Valois, Rob
· *The Lost Legion (Star Wars: The Clone Wars)* – West, Tracey
· *No Prisoners (Star Wars: The Clone Wars)* – Traviss, Karen
· *Star Wars: The Clone Wars* – West, Tracey
· *The Way of the Jedi #1 (Star Wars: The Clone Wars)* – Forbes, Jake

Supernatural

The Winchester brothers battle supernatural threats as hunters. The world at large has no idea these creatures exist, but these two brothers are willing to risk their lives to make humanity safe.

· *Supernatural: The Unholy Cause* – Schreibier, Joe
· *Supernatural: One Year Gone* – Dessetine, Rebecca
· *Supernatural: Night Terror* – Passarella, John
· *Supernatural: War of the Sons* – Dessertine, Rebecca
· *Supernatural: Heart of the Dragon* – Decandido, Keith
· *Supernatural: Witch's Canyon* – Mariotte, Jeff
· *Supernatural: Origins** – *Johntson*, Peter
· *Supernatural Vol.3: Beginning's End** – Dabb, Andrew
· *Supernatural: Rising Son*– Johnston*, Peter

Teenage Mutant Ninja Turtles (various series)

Four turtles mutated into humanoid creatures along with a man mutated into a humanoid rat. The man was a martial arts master and has trained these turtles to be the ultimate ninjas.

· *Teenage Mutant Ninja Turtles Animated Volume 1: Rise of the Turtles** – Sternin, Joshua
· *Teenage Mutant Ninja Turtles: The Ultimate Collection Volume 1** - Eastman, Kevin
· *Teenage Mutant Ninja Turtles Volume 1: Change is Constant (Teenage Mutant Ninja Turtles Graphic Novels)** – Eastman, Kevin
· *Young Samurai: The Way of the Sword* – Bradford, Chris

Teen Wolf

A high-schooler, who is a social outcast, is bitten by a werewolf while looking for a dead girl in the woods. He tries to have a normal life while trying to keep the secret of his furry other side.

· *New Moon* – Meyer, Stephanie
· *On Fire: A Teen Wolf Novel* – Holder, Nancy
· *The Abused Werewolf Rescue Group* – Jinks, Catherine
· *Luna* – Fargo, Gina
· *Ivy Cole and the Moon* – Fargo, Gina
· *The Werewolf Book: The Encyclopedia of Shape-Shifting Beings* – Steiger, Brad

True Blood

True Blood is based on the Charlaine Harris Sookie Stackhouse novels. The books are filled with Vampires, Werewolves, witches and more supernatural goodness.

· *Dead Until Dark* – Harris, Charlaine
· *Living Dead in Dallas* – Harris, Charlaine
· *Club Dead* – Harris, Charlaine
· *Dead to the World* – Harris, Charlaine
· *Dead As a Doornail* – Harris, Charlaine
· *Definitely Dead* – Harris, Charlaine
· *Altogether Dead* – Harris, Charlaine
· *From Dead To Worse* – Harris, Charlaine
· *Dead And Gone* – Harris, Charlaine
· *Dead In The Family* – Harris, Charlaine

- *Dead Reckoning* – Harris, Charlaine
- *Twilight* (series) – Meyer, Stephanie
- *House of Night* (series) – Cast, P.C.
- *The Reformed Vampire Support Group* – Jenkins, Catherin
- *Vampire Diaries* (series) – Smith, L.J.
- *Vampire Kisses* (series) – Schreiber, Ellen

Under the Dome

An invisible dome covers a small town and what follows is the psychological and physical toll it takes on those trap underneath it. It also deals with the ramifications on the outside world and the perceived threat of the dome

- *Under the Dome* – King, Stephen
- *Battle Royal* – Takami, Koushun
- *Lord of the Flies* – Golding, William
- *Life of Pi* – Martel, Yann
- *Hunger Games Trilogy* – Collins, Suzanne
- *Fahrenheit 451* – Bradbury, Ray

V

Lizard Aliens disguised as humans, invade the Earth through false promises and the cloak of friend ship.

- *Ender's Game* – Card, Orson Scott
- *I Am Number Four* – Lore, Pittacus
- *Starship Troopers* – Heinlein, Robert

· *V: The Original Miniseries* – Johnson, Kenneth
· *V: The Second Generation* – Johnson, Kenneth
· *War of the Worlds* – Wells, H.G.

Vampire Diaries

Yet another young adult series turn TV show this time involving the ever popular topic of vampires.

· *Vampire Academy* (*Vampire Academy, Book 1*) – Meed, Richelle
· *Frostbite* (*Vampire Academy, Book 2*) – Meed, Richelle
· *The Vampire Diaries: The Awakening and the Struggle* – Smith L.J.
· *The Vampire Diaries: The Fury and Dark Reunion* – Smith L.J.
· *The Vampire Diaries: The Return: Nightfall* – Smith L.J.
· *The Vampire Diaries: The Return: Shadow Souls* – Smith L.J.
· *The Vampire Diaries: The Return: Midnight* – Smith L.J.
· *Vampire Kisses* (*Vampire Kisses, Book 1*) – Schreiber, Ellen
· *Kissing Coffins* (*Vampire Kisses, Book 2*) – Schreiber, Ellen
· *Secret Circle* (series) – Smith, L.J.
· *Morganville Vampires* (series) – Caine, Rachel

The Walking Dead

The zombies have taken over the world and humanity has fallen into a dystopia. Everyone is looking out for themselves but groups of people band together for survival. Those who have shrived are the true walking dead.

· *The Walking Dead: The Road to Woodbury* – Kirkman, Robert
· *The Walking Dead: The Fall of the Governor* – Kirkman, Robert
· *The Walking Dead Graphic Novel Series** – Kirkman, Robert
· *War World Z* – Brooks, Max
· *Zombie Survival Guide* – Brooks, Max
· *Rotters* – Kraus, Daniel
· *Rot and Ruin* – Maberry, Jonathan
· *Dust & Decay* – Maberry, Jonathan
· *Zom-B* – Shan, Darren

Video Games

Video Games are one of the many things which turned me in an avid reader. What? Video Games helped me learn to read? Yes, because I loved Role Playing Games, which back in the day were very heavily texted based and the dialogue wasn't read aloud to you like they are today. So I had to read and read a lot.

The video games I am going to focus on here are games that have stood the test of time and I am not talking about games like Pac- Man, but games like Final Fantasy or Civilization.

For those you not familiar with video games they do have their own rating scale and just like with movies. If a game is rated "M" for Mature; it doesn't mean Tweens and Teens aren't playing them. Trust me they are. I talk to them all the time at the library about what they are playing.

A lot of people don't realize the amount of reading involved in certain genera of video games or the complex thinking involved with solving puzzles or the complexity of choosing plays in sports games. Video games just aren't Pac-Man eating dots, fruits and blue ghosts.

There is also the chance the teens you are working with don't realize there are books out there based on their favorite video games. So here is your chance catch them off guard with your knowledge of video games.

Types of Games & Examples

FPS – First Person Shooter(s) – *Halo, Gears of War, Call of Duty*

RPG – Role Playing Game – *Final Fantasy, Kingdom Hearts, Elder Scrolls, Pokemon*

Sports - *Madden, FIFA, NBA*

Action/Adventure – *Diablo, Assassin's Creed, Dynasty Warriors, Arkham Asylum, Metal Gear Solid*

Hybrid – Games that combine various types of games – *Borderlands, Mass Effect, God of War*

MMO/MMOG - massively multiplayer online game – *World of Warcraft, Star Wars The Old Republic, DC Universe Online*

Puzzle – *Portal*

Strategy – *Civilization, StarCraft*

Simulation – *Sims*

Rhythm – *Guitar Hero, Rockband*

Platform – *Super Mario Bros., Sonic the Hedgehog, Mega Man*

Assassin's Creed (*1, Brotherhood, 2, Revelations, 3, & 4 Black Flag*)

The game follows the lineage of assassins from the crusades to the Renaissance to the Revolutionary War and to the time of Black Beard and pirates.

· *Assassin's Creed: Forsaken* – Bowden, Oliver
· *Assassin's Creed: Brotherhood* – Bowden, Oliver
· *Assassin's Creed: Renaissance* – Bowden, Oliver
· *Assassin's Creed: The Secret Crusade* – Bowden, Oliver
· *Assassin's Creed: Revelations* – Bowden, Oliver
· *George Washington* (Sterling Biographies) – Calkhoven, Laurie
· Books on the Revolutionary War
· Books on the Crusades
· *Pirates of the Carolinas* – Zepke, Terrance
· *Blackbeard and the Other Pirates of the Atlantic Coast* – Roberts, Nancy

Batman Arkham Asylum/City/Origins

Batman faces off with the Joker and many other of his rouges gallery within the confines of Arkham Asylum.

· *Arkham Asylum: Madness** – Kieth, Sam
· *Batman: Arkham City** – Dini, Paul
· *Batman: Arkham Asylum** – Morrison, Grant
· *Batman: The Killing Joke** – Moore, Alan
· *Batman: The Dark Knight Returns* – Miller, Frank

Borderlands (series)

Vault hunters seek the ultimate treasure hidden within the Vault(s)!

· *Borderlands: Origins** – Neumann, Mikey
· *Borderlands: The Fallen* – Shirley, John
· *Borderlands #2: Unconquered* – Shirley, John
· *Borderland: Gunsight* – Shirley, John

Call of Duty Series (Black Ops, Modern Warfare)

One of the preemie first person shooter war games in the video game world set in the real world.

· *Code Talker: A Novel About the Navajo Marines of World War Two* – Bruchac, Joesph
· *Inside Delta Force: The Story of America's Elite Counterterrorist Unit* – Haney, Eric
· *The Red Badge of Courage* – Crane, Stephen
· *Tom Clancy's Ghost Recon* – Michaels, David
· *Tom Clancy's Ghost Recon: Combat Ops* – Michaels, David
· *Tomorrow, When the War Began (The Tomorrow Series #1)* – Marsden, John

Civilization

Not all video games exist in violence; *Civilization* is a game of strategy, of building up a civilization from the ground up at the Stone Age all the way through the space age. Players take control of one of the famous empires of the world and win through a variety of conditions. This game was created by the legendary Sid Meier.

· *The Age of Wonder: How the Romantic Generation Discovered the Beauty and Terror of Science* – Holmes, Richard
· *Explorers Who Got Lost* – Sansevere– Dreher, Diane
· *The New Penguin History of the World: Fifth Edition* – Roberts, J.M.
· *A Little History of the World* – Gombrich, E.H.
· *Nation* – Pratchett, Terry

DC Universe Online

The player finally gets a chance to fight alongside their favorite villains and heroes of the DC Universe in this MMORPG (massively multiplayer online role-playing game).

· *Brightest Day, Vol.1** – Johns, Geoff
· *Cosmic Odyssey** – Starlin, Jim
· *Crisis of Infinite Earths** – Wolfman, Marv
· *Green Lantern: The Sinestro Corps War, Vol.1** – Johns, Geoff
· *Infinite Crisis** – Johns, Geoff
· *DC Universe Online Legends Vol. 1** – Wolfman, Marv

· *DC Universe Online Legends Vol. 2** – Wolfman, Marv
· *DC Universe Online Legends Vol. 3** – Wolfman, Marv

Dead Rising (series)

Dead Rising, at times, is a comical video game about surviving the zombie apocalypse. This game is produced by CAPCOM.

· *Dead Rising: Road to Fortune** – Waltz, Tom
· *World War Z: An Oral History of the Zombie War* – Brooks, Max
· *The Zombie Survival Guide: Complete Protection from the Living Dead* – Brooks, Max
· *Warm Bodies* – Marion, Issac
· *Zom-B* (series) – Shan, Darren

Dead Space (series)

Horror meets outer space in this first person shooter. You are one of the few survivors on a space station and it is up to you to figure out what is going on and how to save the day.

· *Dead Space** – Johnston, Antony
· *Dead Space: Liberation** – Edginton, Ian
· *Dead Space: Salvage** – Johnston, Antony
· *Dead Space: Catalyst* – Evenson, Brian
· *Dead Space: Martyr* –
· *Aliens Omnibus, Vol. 1** – Verheiden, Mark
· *It* – King, Stephen

Diablo (1,2,3)

This is a dark fantasy game action adventure role playing game, as players go up against Diablo.

· *Birthright (Diablo: The Sin War, Book 1)* – Knaak, Richard
· *Diablo #1: Legacy of Blood* – Knaak, Richard
· *Diablo Archive* – Knaak, Richard
· *Scales of the Serpent (Diablo: The Sin War, Book 2)* – Knaak, Richard
· *The Veiled Prophet (Diablo: The Sin War, Book 3)* – Knaak, Richard

Dragon Age Saga (Dragon Age: Origins, Dragon Age 2)

A hero turned Grey Warden, to battle back the creatures of darkness, the Dark Spawn, an enemy that hadn't been seen in generations. It is now up to this hero, allies, and friends to save the lands.

· *The Calling (Dragon Age)* – Gaider, David
· *The Crystal Shard: The Icewind Dale Trilogy, Part 1)* – Salvatore, R.A.
· *Eye of the World (The Wheel of Time, Book 1)* – Jordan, Robert
· *Dragon Age: the Stolen Throne* – Gaider, David
· *Dragon Age Volume 1* – Card, Orson Scott
· *Dragons of Autumn Twilight (Dragonlance Chronicles, Vol.1)* – Weis, Margaret
· *Lord of the Rings* – Tolkien, J.R.R.

· *Sword of Shannara* – Brooks, Terry

Dynasty Warriors (1,2,3,4,5,6,7,8)

Dynasty Warriors is based on *The Romance of the Three Kingdoms*, a book following the fall of the Han Dynasty to the founding of Jin Dynasty. This is an epic on par with the Odyssey, the Trojan War, King Arthur, and Robin Hood.

· *Le Morte Darthur* – Malory, Sir. Thomas
· *Romance of the Three Kingdoms, Vol.1* – Kuan– Chung, Lo
· *Romance of the Three Kingdoms, Vol.2* – Kuan– Chung, Lo
· *Shogun: A novel of Japan* – Clavell, James
· *The Trojan War: A New History* – Strauss, Barry

Elder Scrolls (Skyrim. Oblivion, Morrowind)

Elder Scrolls is one of the most massively open Role Playing Games out there. It is set in a fantasy world and lets the players pretty much do anything, be anything they want to be.

· *The Elder Scrolls: The Infernal City* – Keyes, Greg
· *Lord of Souls: An Elder Scrolls Novel* – Keyes, Greg
· *Chronicles of the Necromancer* (series) – Martin, Gail Z.
· *Wheel of Time* (series) – Jordan, Robert
· *The Kingkiller Chronicle* (series) – Rothfuss, Patrick

Fable (Fable, Fable II, Fable III)

Fable is an rpg which spans generation all in the same world, so that the player sees how the world has changed over time as technology and civilization builds. You are the hero or villain that shapes the world as the player chooses to help or not to help those that live within the world.

· *Assassin's Creed: Brotherhood* – Bowden, Oliver
· *Assassin's Creed: Renaissance* – Bowden, Oliver
· *The Elder Scrolls: The Infernal City* – Keyes, Greg
· *Fable: The Balverine Order* – David, Peter
· *Lost Souls: An Elder Scrolls Novel* – Keyes, Greg

FIFA (series)

EA's sports game based on international soccer.

· *Soccer Hero* – Christopher, Matt
· *The Soccer Book, Revised Edition* – DK Publishing
· *FIFA World Soccer Records 2012* – Radnedge, Keir
· *Soccer Skills & Drills* – National Soccer Coaches Association of America
· *Soccer Duel* – Christopher, Matt
· *World Cup* – Christopher, Matt
· *DK Biography: Pele* – Buckley, James

Final Fantasy

Final Fantasy is one of the longest running fantasy RPGs of all time. These are worlds filled with monsters, magic, technology, wars, politics, romance and more. There is a reason why these games have survived the test of time.

· *Dawn: The Worlds of Final Fantasy* – Amano, Yoshitaka
· *Dragonriders of Pern* – McCaffrey, Anne
· *Dune–* Herbert, Frank
· *Eye of the World (The Wheel of Time, Book 1)* – Jordan, Robert
· *Nausicaa of the Valley of the Wind* – Miyazaki, Hayao
· *Sword of Shannara* – Brooks, Terry
· *Time of the Twins (Dragonlance: Legends Trilogy)* – Weis, Margaret
· *Vampire Hunter D, Vol.1* – Kikuchi, Hideyuki

Gears of War (series)

Gears of War is a military science fiction third-person shooter. The game focuses on Delta Squad as they attempt a last-ditch effort to save the remaining humans on Sera from Locust Horde.

· *Gears of War: The Slab* – Traviss, Karen
· *Gears of War: Aspho Fields* – Traviss, Karen
· *Gears of War: Coalition's End* – Traviss, Karen
· *Gears of War: Jacinto's Remnant* – Traviss, Karen
· *Gears of War: Anvil Gate* – Traviss, Karen
· *Gears of War, Vol. 1** – Ortega, Joshua

· *Gears of War, Vol. 2** – Ortega, Joshua
· *Gears of War Book Three: Dirty Little Secrets** – Traviss, Karen

God of War (series)

Kratos is a Spartan warrior who serves the Gods and Goddess of Olympus. The goddess Athena tasks Kratos with killing Ares, the God of War, who is responsible for Kratos accidentally killing his family.

· *Mythology* – Hamilton, Edith
· *300** – Miller, Frank
· *God of War* – Stover, Matthew
· *God of War** – Wolfman, Marv
· *God of War II* – Vardeman, Robert
· *On Sparta* – Plutarch

Gran Turismo

Gran Turismo is a racing game of the highest caliber. It is the most realistic racing game out there, letting the player race over 200 different cars from around the world and years.

· *Driving with the Devil: Southern Moonshine Detroit Wheels and the Birth of NASCAR* – Thompson, Neal
· *Inside IMSA's Legendary GTP Race Cars: The Prototype Experience* – Martin, J.A.
· *Legendary Race Cars* – Wasef, Basem
· *Saturday Night Dirt: A MOTOR novel* – Weaver, Will

Guitar Hero/Rockband

Guitar Hero and Rockband are to rhythm music based games that have introduced teens to music they might never have heard.

· *The Girl In the Song: The Stories Behind 50 Rock Classics* – Heatley, Michael
· *A Hard Day's Write: The stories Behind Every Beatles Song* – Turner, Steve
· *KISS: Behind the Mask – The Official Authorized Biography* – Leaf, David
· *The Rolling Stone Illustrated History of Rock and Roll: The Definitive History of the Most Important Artists and Their Music* – Rolling Stone Magazine
· *Take a Walk on the Dark Side: Rock and Roll Myths, Legends, and Curses* – Patterson, R. Gary
· *Woodstock: Three Days that Rocked the World* – Evans, Mike

Halo

Master Chief, the Halo, the Flood, the Covenant; the ultimate first person shoot set in the far future. The game has a huge following and is one of the cornerstones of the X-Box gaming library.

· *Halo: Cryptum: Book One of the Forerunner Saga* – Bear, Greg
· *Halo: The Fall of Reach* – Nylund, Eric
· *Halo: First Strike* – Nylund, Eric

- *Halo: Helljumper** – David, Peter
- *Halo: The Flood* – Dietz, William
- *Ghost of Onyx* – Nylund, Eric
- *Halo: Evolutions: Essential Tales of the Halo Universe* – Buckell, Tobias
- *Halo: Contact Harvest* – Staten, Joseph
- *Halo: Evolutions Vol. II: Essential Tales of the Halo Universe* – Various Authors
- *Halo: Uprising** – Bendis, Brian Michael
- *Halo: Blood Line** – Van Lente, Fred
- *Halo: The Cole Protocol* – Buckell, Tobias

Kingdom Hearts (series)

Disney and Squaresoft come together to create one of the most interesting RPGs of all time. The companies combine elements from their franchise. In its essence it is Disney Worlds and characters meeting up with the character with Final Fantasy. The protagonists for this game are all new characters.

- *Kingdom Hearts: Final Mix, Vol. 1** – Amano, Shiro
- *Kingdom Hearts: Final Mix, Vol. 2** – Amano, Shiro
- *Kingdom Hearts II. Vol. 1** – Amano, Shiro
- *Kingdom Hearts II. Vol. 2** – Amano, Shiro
- *Kingdom Hearts: Chain of Memories** - Amano, Shiro
- *Kingdom Hearts 358/2 Days, Vol. 1** – Amano, Shiro

The Last of Us

Joel is crossing across a post-apocalyptic United States in 2033. He is escorting a young girl, Ellie, to the Fireflies, who believe Ellie may be the key to curing an infection that has ravaged the world.

· *I Am Legend* – Matheson, Richard
· *World War Z: An Oral History of the Zombie War* – Brooks, Max
· *Andromeda Strain* – Crichton, Michael
· *The Last of Us (American Dreams)* – Hicks, Faith
· *Y the Last Man** (series) – Vaughan, Brian
· *Contaminated* – Garner, Em

Legend of Zelda

The Legend of Zelda was one of the first action RPGs following the exploits of Link and the Princess Zelda.

· *The Legend of Zelda, Vol.1* – Himekawa, Akira
· *The Legend of Zelda, Vol.2* – Himekawa, Akira
· *The Legend of Zelda, Vol.3: Majora's Mask* – Himekawa, Akira
· *The Legend of Zelda, Vol.4: Oracle of Seasons* – Himekawa, Akira
· *The Legend of Zelda, Vol.5: Oracle of Ages* – Himekawa, Akira
·*The Legend of Zelda, Vol.6: Four Swords – Part 1* – Himekawa, Akira

·*The Legend of Zelda, Vol.7: Four Swords – Part 2* – Himekawa, Akira
·*The Legend of Zelda, Vol.8: The Minish Cap* – Himekawa, Akira
·*The Legend of Zelda, Vol.9: A Link to the Past* – Himekawa, Akira
·*The Legend of Zelda, Vol.10: Phantom Hour Glass* – Himekawa, Akira

Madden

Madden by EA Sports is the premier football video game.

· *Brett Favre* – Koestler– Grack, Rachel
· *Football Hero* – Green, Tim
· *Football: How It Works (The Science of Sports)* – Biskup, Aqnieska
· *Football Genius* – Green, Tim
· *Knights of the Hill Country* – Tharp, Tim
· *Manning* – Manning, Peyton

Mass Effect (series)

Commander Shepard is on a mission to save the galaxy from a race of mechanical beings known as the Reapers in this hybrid FPS/RPG.

· *Mass Effect Vol. 1** – Walters, Mac
· *Mass Effect Vol. 3: Invasion** – Walters, Mac
· *Mass Effect Vol. 4: Homeworlds** – Walters, Mac

· *Mass Effect: Evolution** – Walters, Mac
· *Mass Effect: Redemption* – Walters, Mac
· *Mass Effect: Revelation* – Karpyshyn, Drew
· *Mass Effect: Ascension* – Karpyshyn, Drew

Mega Man

Mega Man was a robot built to protect humanity from the evil robots of Doctor Wily.

· *Mega Man Megamix Volume 1** – Ariga, Hitoshi
· *Mega Man Megamix Volume 2** – Ariga, Hitoshi
· *Mega Man Megamix Volume 3** – Ariga, Hitoshi
· *Mega Man Gigamix Volume 1** – Ariga, Hitoshi
· *Astro Boy Vol. 1 & 2** – Tezuka, Osamu
· *Astro Boy Vol. 3** – Tezuka, Osamu
· *Astro Boy Vol. 4** – Tezuka, Osamu

Metal Gear Solid (series)

Special Forces operative Solid Snake is assigned to find the "Metal Gear", which is a bipedal walking tank with the ability to launch nuclear weapons.

· *Metal Gear Solid Omnibus** – Oprisko, Kris
· *Metal Gear Solid* – Benson, Raymond
· *Metal Gear Solid: Guns of the Patriot* – Project Itoh
· *Metal Gear Solid 2: The Novel: Sons of Liberty* – Benson, Raymond
· *Tom Clancy's Ghost Recon* – Michaels, David

· *Tom Clancy's Ghost Recon: Combat Ops* – Michaels, David

Mortal Kombat (series)

Martial artists from this world and Out World do battle to decide the fate of the Earth.

· *Dragon Ball Z, Vol. 1 (Dragonball Z Vizbig Editions)* – Toriyama, Akira
· *Dragon Ball Z, Vol. 2 (Dragonball Z Vizbig Editions)* – Toriyama, Akira
· *Shaman King, Vol.1: A Shaman in Tokyo* – Takei, Hiroyuki
· *Shaman King Vol.2: Kung– Fu Master – Takei, Hiroyuki*
· *YuYu Hakusho, Vol. 1 – Togashi, Yoshihiro*
· *YuYu Hakusho, Vol. 2 – Togashi, Yoshihiro*

NBA Live

EA sports premier NBA basketball game.

· *The Art of a Beautiful Game: The Thinking Fan's Tour of the NBA* – Ballard, Chris
· *Hoops* – Myers, Walter Dean
· *Slam!* – Myers, Walter Dean
· *Playing for Keeps: Michael Jordan and the World He Made* – Halberstam, David

Pokemon

"Gotta Catch Them All," the catch phrase for Pokemon, a throwback to old school 8-bit video game RPGs. There are two goals to this game one to become the Champion of the Pokemon League and two to catch all the different Pokemon that exist in the world. While all of this is going on it is up to the hero to defeat an evil organization from ruling the world. There are lots and lots of Pokemon books out there; this is only a small sampling of those out there.

· *Pokemon Adventures, Vol.1* – Kusaka, Hidenori
· *Pokemon Adventures, Vol.2*– Kusaka, Hidenori
· *Pokemon Adventures, Vol.3* – Kusaka, Hidenori
· *Pokemon Adventures, Vol.4* – Kusaka, Hidenori
· *Pokemon Adventures, Vol.5* – Kusaka, Hidenori
· *Pokemon Adventures, Vol.6* – Kusaka, Hidenori
· *Pokemon Adventures, Vol.7* – Kusaka, Hidenori
· *Pokemon Adventures, Vol.8* – Kusaka, Hidenori
· *Pokemon Adventures, Vol.9* – Kusaka, Hidenori
· *Pokemon Adventures, Vol.10* – Kusaka, Hidenori
· *Pokemon: Diamond and Pearl Adventure!, Vol. 1* – Ihara, Shigekatsu
· *Pokemon: Diamond and Pearl Adventure!, Vol. 2* – Ihara, Shigekatsu
· *Pokemon: Diamond and Pearl Adventure!, Vol. 3* – Ihara, Shigekatsu
· *Pokemon Adventures: Diamond and Pearl/Platinum Vol. 1* – Kusaka, Hidenori
· *Pokemon Adventures: Diamond and Pearl/Platinum Vol. 2* – Kusaka, Hidenori

Portal (series)

Portal 2 is a first-person perspective puzzle game. Players take the role of Chell. The game is a series of puzzles which must be solved by teleporting the player's character and simple objects using the portal gun.

· *Valve Presents: The Sacrifice and Other Steam-Powered Stories Volume 1** – Valve
· *Physics of the Impossible: A Scientific Exploration into the World of Phasers, Force Fields, Teleportation, and Time Travel* – Kaku, Michio
· *I, Robot* – Asimov, Isaac
· *Robot Visions* – Asimov, Isaac
· *The Invention of Hugo Cabret* – Selznick, Brian
· *Hitchhiker's Guide to the Galaxy* – Adams, Douglas

Red Dead Redemption

Red Dead Redemption brought westerns to the video game world in an amazing way in this sandbox game.

· *The Authentic Life of Billy the Kid* – Garrett, Pat F.
· *Last of the Mohicans* – Cooper, James
· *The Lone Ranger trade paperback** – Mathews, Brett
· *The Mark of Zorro* – McCulley, Johnston
· *Shane* – Schaefer, Jack
· *True Grit* – Portis, Charles

Resident Evil (series)

This series is about the "The Zombie Apocalypse" and the band of heroes trying to save the day. Any of the pervious entries about zombies will also do for books that might interest teens who are interested in this game series.

· *Resident Evil Archives* (series) – BradyGames
· *Resident Evil: The Umbrella Conspiracy* – Perry, S.D.
· *Resident Evil: Underworld* – Perry, S.D.
· *Resident Evil: City of the Dead* – Perry, S.D.
· *Resident Evil: Caliban Cove* – Perry, S.D.
· *Resident Evil: Nemesis* – Perry, S.D.
· *Resident Evil: Zero Hour* – Perry, S.D.
· *Resident Evil: Code Veronica* – Perry, S.D.
· *Resident Evil: Retribution - The Official Movie Novelization* – Shirley, John

Smack Down/Raw/Wrestling

These are wrestling games based on the various wrestling groups which exist and have existed. The thing about biographies for the various wrestlers out there; they are either adult or child and not really focused on Tweens and Teens. I am going to focus on the younger reader books here because of the use of photographs and making the books more action packed.

· *Ric Flair: The Story of the Wrestler They Call "The Nature Boy"* – Hunter, Matt

· *The Story of the Wrestler They Call "Hollywood" Hulk Hogan* – Hunter, Matt
· *The Story of the Wrestler They Call "The Undertaker"* – Ross, Dan
· *Jesse Venture: the Story of the Wrestler they call "The Body"* – Hunter, Matt
· *Bill Goldberg* – Alexander, Kyle
· *The Women of Pro Wrestling* – Alexander, Kyle
· *Pro Wrestling's Greatest Tag Teams* – Hunter, Matt
· *Randy Savage: the Story of the Wrestler They Call "Macho Man"* – Mudge, Jaccqueline
· *Pro Wrestling's Greatest Wars*
· *The Story of the Wrestler They Call "Sting"* – Alexander, Kyle
· *Steve Austin: the Story of the Wrestler they call "Stone Cold"* – Ross, Dan

Sonic the Hedgehog

Where Nintendo had Mario as their mascot; SEGA had a super-fast blue hedgehog, Sonic.

· *Sonic the Hedgehog Archives 1* – Spazinate, Patrick
· *Sonic the Hedgehog Archives 2* – Spazinate, Patrick
· *Sonic the Hedgehog Archives 3* – Spazinate, Patrick
· *Sonic the Hedgehog Select Vol. 1* – Gallagher, Mike
· *Sonic the Hedgehog Select Vol. 2* – Various
· *Sonic the Hedgehog Select Vol. 3* – Flynn, Ian

StarCraft

This is Blizzards turn based space combat game. There are three different factions the Human based Space Marines, the alien monsters Zerg and the highly evolved and technologically based Protoss.

· *Firstborn (StarCraft: Dark Templar, Book 1)* – Golden, Christie
· *Grey Knights: The Omnibus* – Counter, Ben
· *Mass Effect: Deception* – Dietz, William
· *Mass Effect: Retribution* – Karpyshyn, Drew
· *The Ultramarines Omnibus* – McNeill, *Graham*
· *Starcraft: Queen of Blades* – Rosenberg, Aaron
· *The Starcraft Archive: An Anthology* – Grubb,Jeff
· *Starcraft II: Heaven's Devils* – Dietz, William
· *Starcraft II: Devil's Due* – Golden, Christie

Star Wars (Knights of the Old Republic, The Force Unleashed, The Old Republic)

Star Wars turned in to video games of all shapes and sizes. See also all the other entries based on the Star Wars Universe.

· *Star Wars: Darth Bane: Dynasty of Evil: A novel of the Old Republic* – Karpshyn, Drew
· *Star Wars: The Force Unleashed* – Williams, Sean
· *Star Wars: The Force Unleashed II* – Williams, Sean
· *Star Wars: Knights of the Old Republic, Vol.1** – Miller, John

· *Star Wars: Knights of the Old Republic, Vol.2** – Miller, John
· *Star Wars: The Old Republic: Fatal Alliance* – Williams, Sean
· *Star Wars: The Old Republic: Deceived* – Kemp, Paul
· *Star Wars: The Old Republic Volume 1 – Blood of the Empire** – Freed, Alexander

Super Mario Bros. (Donkey Kong, Paper Mario, Dr. Mario, Mario Kart, etc.)

Mario quickly became the mascot of Nintendo dating all the way back to the Donkey Kong Arcade Machine.

· *Super Mario: How Nintendo Conquered America* – Ryan, Jeff
· *Nintendo Magic: Winning the Videogame Wars* – Inoue, Osamu
· *Vintage Games: An Insider Look at the History of Grand Theft Auto, Super Mario, and the Most Influential Games of All Time* – Loguidice, Bill
· *Extra Lives: Why Video Games Matter* – Bissell, Tom
· *1001 Video Games You Must Play Before You Die* – Mott, Tony

Tomb Raider (series)

Lara Croft an archeologist of renowned ability. The female Indian Jones set in the modern age.

· *Indiana Jones* (novels) – McCoym Max
· *Indiana Jones Omnibus, Vol.1** – Loeb-Messner, William
· *Indiana Jones and the Raiders of the Lost Ark* – Black, Campbell
· *Indiana Jones and the Last Crusade* – Macgregor, Rob
· *Uncharted: The Fourth Labyrinth* – Golden, Christopher
· *Tomb Raider, Vol. 2: Mystic Artifacts* – Jurgens, Dan
· *Archaeology for Dummies* – White, Nancy

Ultimate Alliance 1 & 2 (Marvel)

Marvel Ultimate Alliance lets you play as any number of heroes and villains straight from the pages of Marvel Comics.

· *Avengers: The Contest (Marvel Premiere Classic)* – Mantlo, Bill
· *Avengers Disassembled* – Bendis, Brian Michael
· *Infinity Gauntlet* – Starlin, Jim
· *Civil War* – Millar, Mark
· *Siege* – Bendis, Brian Michael

Uncharted (series)

The series follows modern-day treasure hunter Nathan "Nate" Drake and his adventures to uncover wondrous treasures.

· *Uncharted** - Williamson, Joshua
· *Uncharted: The Fourth Labyrinth* – Golden, Christopher
· *Drake's Journal Inside the Making of Uncharted 3* –
North, Nolan
· Dirk Pitt Adventures (series) – Cussler, Clive
· Robert Langdon Adventures (series) – Brown, Dan

WarCraft

Warcraft was once a fantasy turn based strategy game but was transformed into the largest and most popular MMO of all time.

· *Warcraft Archive* – Knaak, Richard
· *Warcraft War of the Ancients Archive* – Knaak, Richard
· *World of Warcraft: the Shattering: Prelude to the Cataclysm* – Golden, Christine
· *World of Warcraft: Arthas; Rise of the Lich King* –
Golden, Christine
· *World of Warcraft: Chronicles of War* – Golden,
Christine

Other Resources

First I just want to say; what I give you in this book is only a small sliver of what is out there in the world of movies, TV shows and video games. I could fill pages upon pages of a book if I tried to do every movie, TV show, or video game out there. They would each also have to be separate volumes. Plus there is the teen and tween factor of what is current and a trend. Just think back to when you were a teen and what you liked and thought was cool; do you think it would be relevant to the teens of today? That is the thing about pop culture it is constantly evolving, changing like a living organism and I think that is one of the amazing things about it. And at times it is hard to keep up with.

Even though the worlds of teen and tween interests are always changing it doesn't mean you have to be left out in the dark without some guidance past this book. There are some wonderful online resources in which I use when I am stumped or have missed something I should know about. I freely admit my knowledge of music and sports is lacking. So I have to look for help myself and I do turn to the trusted internet.

IMDB (internet movie data base) – imdb.com – like I said earlier, IMDB is a wonderful site that gives you plot summaries of TV shows and movies. It also lists actors, actress, directors, etc. and it even has bits of trivia about whatever you are looking up.

Library Thing – librarything.com – this hands down is one of my favorite sites when trying to find a book. The unique thing about this site is that has user created content in the form of tags. Tags are basically keywords the reader thinks of about the book and the reader definitely has a different perspective on these keywords than a librarian does. But tags only work if you have a large enough sampling of people providing this data, otherwise it fails. Lucky enough Library Thing has enough people who love books generating these tags. Libraries all around the world are tying their own catalogues into Library Things just for the use of these tags and helping their patrons find books in their own system.

Library Thing also generates list of possible books one might like to read next and readers are also allowed to help generate these lists. Take an afternoon, if you aren't already using Library Thing, to familiarize yourself with all it can provide you.

Gamespot – gamespot.com – is one of the best websites out there for information on video games; new, old, and coming soon. It gives reviews, summaries, and news to keep you to date on the world of video games.

Gameinformer – gameinformer.com – is another great website for news on upcoming video games releases and news. It is owned by Game Stop the largest retail chain devoted to selling new and used video games and systems.

Newsarama – newsarama.com – is a website that does a really great job bringing together all comic book related news being released from the various companies from story lines to TV/movie news to video games. If it is comic book related you can find it here.

Diamond Comic Distributors – diamondcomics.com – Diamond is the largest distributor of comics and graphic novels out there. I like looking at their sale charts to make sure I haven't missed a graphic novel or TPB I should have picked up for my collection.

Amazon – amazon.com – Amazon does a great job in breaking down categories in a variety of different ways to let you see what is coming out and what people are buying and interested in. Again I come here to double check I haven't missed something the Teens are reading and that I might have over looked.

Index

The index present here covers Movies, TV Shows, and Video Game titles. So you can quickly scan the index to see if a tween or teen mentions a title to you.

#

A

B

C

D

E

F

G

H

K

L

M

N

O

P

T

X

Z

www.ingramcontent.com/pod-product-compliance
Lightning Source LLC
Chambersburg PA
CBHW070205060426
42445CB00033B/1551